CLASSIC SERMONS
ON THE
SEASONS OF LIFE

CLASSIC SERMONS ON THE SEASONS OF LIFE

Compiled by

Warren W. Wiersbe

kregel
PUBLICATIONS

Grand Rapids, MI 49501

Classic Sermons on the Seasons of Life
Compiled by Warren W. Wiersbe

Published by Kregel Publications, a division of Kregel, Inc.,
P.O. Box 2607, Grand Rapids, MI 49501. Kregel Publications provides trusted, biblical publications for Christian
growth and service. Your comments and suggestions are
valued.

For more information about Kregel Publications, visit our
web site at http://www.kregel.com.

Cover photo: Patricia Sgrignoli, POSITIVE IMAGES
Cover and book design: Alan G. Hartman

Library of Congress Cataloging-in-Publication Data
Classic sermons on the seasons of life / Warren W.
Wiersbe, compiler
     p.   cm.— (Kregel classic sermons series)
  Includes index.
    1. Sermons, English. 2. Sermons, English—Scotland
3. Sermons, American. I. Wiersbe, Warren W. II. Series.
BV4253.C57   1997   252—dc21   97-28850
                                         CIP

ISBN   0-8254-4079-3

Printed in the United States of America

1 2 3 / 03 02 01 00 99 98 97

CONTENTS

LIST OF SCRIPTURE TEXTS

PREFACE

THE *KREGEL CLASSIC SERMONS SERIES* is an attempt to assemble and publish meaningful sermons from master preachers about significant themes.

These are *sermons,* not essays or chapters taken from books about themes. Not all of these sermons could be called great, but all of them are *meaningful.* They apply the truths of the Bible to the needs of the human heart, which is something that all effective preaching must do.

While some are better known than others, all of the preachers whose sermons I have selected had important ministries and were highly respected in their day. The fact that a sermon is included in this volume does not mean that either the compiler or the publisher agrees with or endorses everything that the man did, preached, or wrote. The sermon is here because it has a valued contribution to make.

These are sermons about *significant* themes. The pulpit is no place to play with trivia. The preacher has thirty minutes in which to help mend broken hearts, change defeated lives, and save lost souls; he can never accomplish this demanding ministry by distributing homiletical tidbits. In these difficult days we do not need clever pulpiteers who discuss the times; we need dedicated ambassadors who will preach the eternities.

The reading of these sermons can enrich your spiritual life. The studying of them can enrich your skills as an interpreter and expounder of God's truth. However God uses these sermons in your life and ministry, my prayer is that His church around the world will be encouraged and strengthened by them.

WARREN W. WIERSBE

The Bitterness and Blessedness of the Brevity of Life

Alexander Maclaren (1826–1910) was one of Great Britain's most famous preachers. While pastoring the Union Chapel, Manchester (1858–1903), he became known as "the prince of expository preachers." Rarely active in denominational or civic affairs, Maclaren invested his time in studying the Word in the original languages and sharing its truths with others in sermons that are still models of effective expository preaching. He published a number of books of sermons and climaxed his ministry by publishing his monumental *Expositions of Holy Scripture.*

This message was taken from *Sermons Preached in Manchester,* Third Series, published in 1902 by Funk and Wagnalls, New York.

Alexander Maclaren

1

THE BITTERNESS AND BLESSEDNESS OF THE BREVITY OF LIFE

Surely every man walketh in a vain shew. . . . I am a stranger with thee, and a sojourner, as all my fathers were (Psalm 39:6, 12).

THESE TWO SAYINGS are two different ways of putting the same thing. There is a common thought underlying both, but the associations with which that common thought is connected in these two verses are distinctly different. The one is bitter and sad—a gloomy half truth. The other, out of the very same fact, draws blessedness and hope. The one may come from no higher point of view than the level of worldly experience; the other is a truth of faith. The former is at best partial, and without the other may be harmful; the latter completes, explains, and hallows it.

And that this progress and variety in the thought is the key to the whole psalm is, I think, obvious to anyone who will examine it with care. I cannot here enter on that task but in the hastiest fashion by way of vindicating the connection which I trace between the two verses of our text. The psalmist begins, then, with telling how at some time recently passed—in consequence of personal calamity not very clearly defined, but apparently some bodily sickness aggravated by mental sorrow and anxiety—he was struck dumb with silence so that he held his peace even from good. In that state there rose within him many sad and miserable thoughts, which at last force their way through his locked lips. They shape themselves into a prayer which is more complaint than petition and is absorbed in the contemplation of the manifest melancholy facts of human life: "Thou hast made my days as an hand-breadth; and mine age is as nothing before thee." And then, as that thought dilates and sinks deeper into his soul, he looks out upon the whole race of man and, in tones of bitterness and hopelessness, affirms that all are vanity, shadows, disquieted in vain. The blank hopelessness of such a view brings him to a standstill. It is true, but taken alone is too dreadful to think of. "That way madness lies," so he breaks short off his almost despairing thoughts. With a swift turning away of his mind from the downward gaze into blackness that was beginning to make him reel, he fixes his eyes on the throne above: "And now, LORD, what wait I for? my hope is in thee."

These words form the turning point of the psalm. After them, the former thoughts are repeated, but with what a difference—made by looking at all the blackness and sorrow, both personal and universal, in the bright light of that hope which streams upon the most lurid masses of opaque cloud until their gloom begins to glow with an inward luster and softens into solemn purples and reds. He had said, "I was dumb with silence—even from good." But when his hope is in God, the silence changes its character and becomes resignation and submission. "I opened not my mouth; because thou didst it." The variety of human life and its transiency is not less plainly seen than before. But in the light of that hope it is regarded in reference to God's paternal correction and is seen to be the consequence not of a defect in His creative wisdom or love but of man's sin. "Thou with rebukes dost correct man for iniquity." That, to him who waits on the Lord, is the reason and the alleviation of the reiterated conviction "every man is vanity." Not any more does he say every man "at his best state," or, as it might be more accurately expressed, "even when most firmly established." The man who is established in the Lord is not vanity but only the man who founds his being on the fleeting present.

Then, things being so, life being thus in itself and apart from God so fleeting and so sad, and yet a hope that brightens it like sunshine through an April shower brings the psalmist to rise to prayer, in which that formerly expressed conviction of the brevity of life is reit-

erated with the addition of two words which changes its
whole aspect: "I am a stranger *with thee.*" He is God's
guest in his transient life. It is short, like the stay of a
foreigner in a strange land. But he is under the care of
the King of the land, therefore he need not fear nor sorrow. Past generations, Abraham, Isaac, and Jacob—
whose names God "is not ashamed" to appeal to in His
own solemn designation of Himself—have held the same
relation, and their experience has sealed His faithful care
of those who dwell with Him. Therefore, the sadness is
soothed, and the vain and fleeting life of earth assumes
a new appearance. The most blessed and wisest issue of
our consciousness of frailty and insufficiency is the fix-
ing of our desires and hopes on Him in whose house we
may dwell even while we wander to and fro, and in whom
our life being rooted and established shall not be vain,
howsoever it may be brief.

If, then, we follow the course of contemplation thus
traced in the psalm, we have these three points brought
before us: first, the thought of life common to both
clauses; second, the gloomy, aimless hollowness which
that thought breathes into life apart from God; third, the
blessedness which springs from the same thought when
we look at it in connection with our Father in heaven.

The Thought of Life Common to Both Verses

Observe the very forcible expression which is given
here to the thought of life common to both verses: "Every
man walketh in a vain show." The original is even more
striking and strong. And although one does not like
altering words so familiar as those of our translation—
which have sacredness from association and a
melancholy music in their rhythm—still it is worthwhile
to note that the force of the expression which the psalmist
employs is correctly given in the margin, "in an image"
or "in a shadow." The phrase sounds singular to us but
is an instance of a common enough Hebrew idiom. It is
equivalent to saying "he walks in the character or
likeness of a shadow"; or, as we should say, "he walks as
a shadow." That is to say, the whole outward life and

activity of every man is represented as fleeting and unsubstantial, like the reflection of a cloud that darkens leagues of the mountain's side in a moment, and "ere a man can say, behold," is gone again forever.

Then, look at the other image employed in the other clause of our text to express the same idea: "I am a stranger and a sojourner, as all my fathers." The phrase has a history. In that most pathetic narrative of an old-world sorrow long since calmed and consoled, when "Abraham stood up from before his dead" and craved a burying place for his Sarah from the sons of Heth, his first plea was, "I am a stranger and a sojourner with you." In his lips it was no metaphor. He was a stranger, a visitor for a brief time to an alien land. He was a sojourner, having no rights of inheritance, but settled among them for awhile, and, though dwelling among them, not adopted into their community. He was a foreigner, not naturalized. And such is our relation to all this visible frame of things in which we dwell. It is alien to us. Though we be in it, our true affinities are elsewhere; though we be in it, our stay is brief, as that of "a wayfaring man that turns aside to tarry for a night."

And there is given in the context still another metaphor setting forth the same fact in that dreary generalization that precedes my text: "Every man at his best state" or, as the word means, "established," with his roots most firmly struck in the material and visible—"is only a breath." It appears for a moment, curling from lip and nostril into the cold morning air, and vanishes away. So then, vaporous, filmy is the seeming solid fact of the most stable life.

These have been the commonplaces of poets and rhetoricians and moralists in all time. But threadbare as the thought is, I may venture to dwell on it for a moment. I know I am only repeating what we all believe—and all forget. It is never too late to preach commonplaces until everybody acts on them as well as admits them—and this old familiar truth has not yet gotten so wrought into the structure of our lives that we can afford to say no more about it.

"Surely every man walketh in a shadow." Did you ever stand upon the shore on some day of that "uncertain weather, when gloom and glory meet together," and notice how swiftly there went racing over miles of billows a darkening that quenched all the play of color in the waves, as if all of a sudden the angel of the waters had spread his broad wings between sun and sea. Then how in another moment as swiftly it flits away, and with a burst the light blazes out again, and leagues of ocean flash into green and violet and blue. So fleeting, so utterly perishable are our lives for all their seeming solid permanency. "Shadows in a career," as George Herbert has it—breath going out of the nostrils. We think of ourselves as ever to continue in our present posture. We are deceived by illusions. Mental indolence, a secret dislike of the thought, and the impostures of sense all conspire to make us blind to, or at least oblivious of, the plain fact that every beat of our pulses might preach and the slow creeping hands of every parish clock confirm. How awful that silent, unceasing footfall of receding days is when once we begin to watch it!

Inexorable, passionless—though hope and fear may pray, "Sun, stand thou still on Gibeon; and thou moon, in the valley of Ajalon"—the tramp of the hours goes on. The poets paint them as a linked chorus of rosy forms, garlanded and clasping hands as they dance onward. So they may be to some of us at some moments. So they may seem as they approach. But those who come hold the hands of those who go. That troop has no rosy light upon their limbs, their garlands are faded, the sunshine falls not upon the gray and shrouded shapes as they steal ghostlike through the gloom—and ever and ever the bright and laughing sisters pass on into that funereal band which grows and moves away from us unceasing. Alas for many of us it bears away with it our lost treasures, our battered hopes, our joys, from which all the bright petals have dropped! Alas! for many of us there is nothing but sorrow in watching how all things become "part and parcel of the dreadful past."

And how strangely sometimes even a material

association may give new emphasis to that old threadbare truth. Some more permanent *thing* may help us to feel more profoundly the shadowy fleetness of *man*. The trifles are so much more lasting than their owners. Or, as "the preacher" puts it with such wailing pathos, "One generation passeth away, and another generation cometh, but the earth abideth for ever." This material is perishable—but yet how much more enduring than we are!

The pavements we walk upon, the coals in our grates—how many millenniums old are they? The pebble you kick aside with your foot—how many generations will it outlast? Go into a museum and you will see hanging there, little the worse for centuries, battered shields, notched swords, and gaping helmets. Aye, but what has become of the bright eyes that once flashed the light of battle through the bars, what has become of the strong hands that once gripped the hilts? "The knights are dust," and "their good swords are" *not* "rust." The material lasts after its owner. Seed corn is found in a mummy case. The poor form beneath the painted lid is brown and hard, and more than half of it gone to pungent powder. The man that once lived has faded utterly, but the handful of seed has its mysterious life in it. When it is sown, in due time the green blade pushes above English soil, as it would have done under the shadow of the pyramids four thousand years ago. Its produce waves in a hundred harvest fields today. The money in your purses now bears the heads of presidents that died half a century ago. It is bright and useful—where are all the people that in turn said they "owned" it? Other men will live in our houses, will preach from this pulpit, and sit in these pews when you and I are far away. Other June days will come, and the old rosebushes will flower around houses where unborn men will then be living when the present possessor is gone to nourish the roots of the roses in the graveyard!

"Our days are as a shadow, and there is none abiding." So said David on other occasions. We know how true it is, whether we consider the ceaseless flux and change of things, the mystic march of the silent-footed hours, or the greater permanence that attaches to the "things which perish," than to our abode among them. We know it. Yet how hard it is not to yield to the inducement to act and feel as if all this painted scenery were solid rock and mountain. By our own inconsiderateness and sensuousness, we live in a lie, in a false dream of permanence. So in a sadder sense we walk in "a vain shew," deluding ourselves with the conceit of durability and refusing to see that the apparent is the shadowy, and the one enduring reality God. It is hard to get even the general conviction vivified in men's minds, hardest of all to get any man to reflect upon it as applying to himself.

Do not think that you have said enough to vindicate neglect of my words now when you call them commonplace. So they are. But did you ever take that well-worn, old story and press it on your own consciousness—as a man might press a common little plant, whose juice is healing, against his dim eyeball—by saying to yourself, "It is true of *me. I* walk as a shadow. *I* am gliding onward to my doom. Through *my* slack hands the golden sands are flowing. Soon *my* hourglass will run out, and *I* shall have to stop and go away." Let me beseech you for one half-hour's meditation on that fact before this day closes. You will forget my words then, when with your own eyes you have looked upon that truth and felt that it is not merely a toothless commonplace but belongs to and works in *thy* life—as it ebbs away silently and incessantly from *thee.*

The Hollowness Which That Thought, Apart from God, Infuses Into Life

There is, no doubt, a double idea in the metaphor which the psalmist employs. He desires to set forth, by his image of a shadow, not only the transiency but the unsubstantialness of life. Shadow is opposed to substance, to that which is real, as well as that which is enduring. We may further say that the one of these characteristics is in great part the occasion of the other. Because life is fleeting, therefore, in part, it is so hollow and unsatisfying. The fact that men are dragged away from their pursuits so inexorably makes these pursuits seem, to anyone who cannot see beyond that fact, trivial and not worth the doing. Why should we fret and toil and break our hearts—"and scorn delights, and live laborious days"—for purposes that will last so short a time, and things that we shall so soon have to leave? What is all the bustle and business when the sad light of that thought falls on it, but "labouring for the wind"? "Were it not better to lie still?"

Such thoughts have at least a partial truth in them, and are difficult to meet as long as we think only of the facts and results of man's life that we can see with our eyes. And our psalm gives emphatic utterance to them. The word rendered "'walketh" in our text is not merely a synonym for passing through life, but has a very striking meaning. It is an intensive frequentative form of the word—that is, it represents the action as being repeated over and over again. For instance, it might be used to describe the restless motion of a wild beast in a cage, raging from side to side, never still and never getting any farther for all the racing backward and forward. So here it signifies "walketh to and fro," and implies hurry and bustle, continuous effort, habitual unrest. It thus comes to be parallel with the stronger words that follow—"Surely they are *disquieted* in vain." One reason why all this effort and agitation are purposeless and sad is because the man who is straining his nerves and wearying his legs is but a shadow in duration—"He heapeth up riches, and knoweth not who shall gather them."

Yes! if we have said all when we have said "men pass as a fleeting shadow"—if my life has no roots in the Eternal nor any consciousness of a life that does not pass and a light that never perishes; if it is derived from, directed to, "cribbed, cabined, and confined" within this visible diurnal sphere—then it is all flat and unprofitable, an illusion while it seems to last. All its pursuits are folly, its hopes dreams, its substances vapors, its years a lie. For, if life be thus short, I who live it am conscious of and possess (whether I be conscious of them or no) capacities and requirements that, though they were to be annihilated tomorrow, could be satisfied while they lasted by nothing short of the absolute ideal, the all-perfect, the infinite—or, to put away abstractions, "My soul thirsteth for God, the living God!" "He hath put eternity in their heart," as the book of Ecclesiastes says. Longings and aspirations, weaknesses and woes, the limits of creature helps and loves, the disproportion between us and the objects around us—all these facts of familiar experience do witness, alike by blank misgivings and by bright hopes, by many disappointments and by indestructible expectations surviving them all, that nothing that has a date, a beginning, or an end, can fill our souls or give us rest. Can you fill up the swamps of the Mississippi with any cart loads of faggots you can fling in? Can you fill your souls with anything which belongs to this fleeting life? Has a flying shadow an appreciable thickness, or will a million of them pressed together occupy a space in your empty, hungry heart?

And so, dear brethren, I come to you with a message which may sound gloomy, and beseech you to give heed to it. No matter how you may get on in the world—though you may fulfill every dream with which you began in your youth—you will certainly find that without Christ for your Brother and Savior, God for your friend, and heaven for your hope, life, with all its fullness, is empty. It lasts long, too long as it sometimes seems for work, too long for hope, too long for endurance. It lasts long enough to make love die, and joys wither and fade, and companions drop away, but without God and Christ, you will find it but as a watch in the night. At no moment through the long weary years will it satisfy your whole being. And when the weary years are all past it will seem to have been but as one troubled moment breaking the eternal silence. At every point *so* profitless, and all the points making so thin and short a line! The crested waves seem heaped together as they recede from the eye until they reach the horizon, where miles of storm are seen but as a line of spray. So when a man looks back upon his life, if it has been a godless one, be sure of this: that it will be a dark and cheerless retrospect over a tossing waste with a white rim of wandering, barren foam vexed by tempest. Then, if not before, he will sadly learn how he has been living amidst shadows and, with a nature that needs God, has wasted himself upon the world. "O life, as futile then as frail." "Surely," in such a case, "every man walketh in a vain shew."

The Blessedness That Springs from This Same Thought of Life When It Is Looked At in Connection with God

The mere conviction of the brevity and hollowness of life is not in itself a religious or a helpful thought. Its power depends upon the other ideas which are associated with it. It is susceptible of the most opposite applications, and may tend to impel conduct in exactly opposite directions. It may be the language of despair or of bright hope. It may be the bitter creed of a worn-out debauchee, who has wasted his life in hunting shadows and is left with a cynical spirit and a bitter tongue. It may be the passionless belief of a retired student or the fanatical faith of a religious ascetic. It may be an argument for sensuous excess: "Let us eat and drink, for tomorrow we die." Or it may be the stimulus for noble and holy living: "I must work the works of Him that sent me while it is day. The night cometh." The connection in which it is held determines whether it shall be a blight or a blessing to a man.

And the one addition which is needed to incline the whole weight of that conviction to the better side, and to light up all its blackness, is that little phrase in this text, "I am a stranger *with thee,* and a sojourner." There seems to be an allusion here to the remarkable words connected with the singular Jewish institution of the Jubilee. You remember that by the Mosaic law there was no absolute sale of land in Israel, but that every half century the whole returned to the descendants of the original occupiers. Important economical and social purposes were contemplated in this arrangement, as well as the preservation of the relative position of the tribes as settled at the conquest. But the law itself assigns a purely religious purpose—the preservation of the distinct consciousness of the tenure on which the people held their territory, namely, obedience to and dependence on God. "The land shall not be sold for ever, for the land is mine, for ye are *strangers and sojourners with me.*" Of course, there was a special sense in which that was true with regard to Israel, but David thought that the words were as true in regard to his whole relation of God, as in regard to Israel's possession of its national inheritance

If we grasp these words as completing all that we have already said, how different this transient and unsubstantial life looks. You must have the light from both sides to stereoscope and make solid the flat surface picture. Transient! yes—but it is passed in the presence of God. Whether we know it or not, our brief days hang upon Him, and we walk, all of us, in the light of His countenance. That makes the transient eternal, the shadowy substantial, the trivial heavy with solemn meaning and awful yet vast possibilities. "In our embers is something that doth live." If we had said all, when we say "We are as a shadow," it would matter very little, though even then it *would* matter something, how we spent our shadowy days. But if these poor brief hours are spent in the great "Taskmaster's eye"—if the shadow cast on earth proclaims a light in the heavens, if from this point there hangs an unending chain of conscious being—oh, then, with what awful solemnity is the brevity, with what tremendous magnitude is the minuteness of our earthly days invested! "With thee"—then I am constantly in the presence of a sovereign law and its Giver; "with thee"— then all my actions are registered and weighed yonder; "with thee"—then "thou, God, seest me." It is the prismatic halo and ring of eternity around this poor glass of time that gives it all its dignity, all its meaning. The lives that are lived before God cannot be trifles.

And if this relation to time be recognized and accepted and held fast by our hearts and minds, then what calm blessedness will flow into our souls!

"A stranger with thee"—then we are the guests of the

King. The Lord of the land charges Himself with our protection and provision. We journey under His safe conduct. It is for His honor and faithfulness that no harm shall come to us traveling in His territory and relying on His Word. Like Abraham with the sons of Heth, we may claim the protection and help that a stranger needs. He recognizes the bond and will fulfill it. We have eaten of His salt, and He will answer for our safety. "He that toucheth you toucheth the apple of mine eye."

"A stranger with thee"—then we have a constant companion and an abiding presence. We may be solitary and necessarily remote from the polity of the land. We may feel amid all the visible things of earth as if foreigners. We may not have a foot of soil, not even a grave for our dead. Companionships may dissolve and warm hands grow cold and their close clasp relax—what then? He is with us still. He will join us as we journey, even when our hearts are sore with loss. He will walk with us by the way and make our chill hearts glow. He will sit with us at the table—however humble the meal—and He will not leave us when we discern Him. Strangers we are indeed here—but not solitary, for we are "strangers with thee." As in some ancestral home in which a family has lived for centuries—son after father has rested in these great chambers and been safe behind the strong walls— so, age after age, they who love Him abide in God. "Thou hast been our dwelling-place in all generations."

"Strangers with thee"— then we may carry our thoughts forward to the time when we shall go to our true home nor wander any longer in the land that is not ours. If even here we come into such blessed relationship with God, that fact is in itself a prophecy of a more perfect communion and a heavenly house. They who are strangers with Him will one day be at "home with the Lord." And in the light of that blessed hope the transiency of this life changes its whole aspect, loses the last trace of sadness, and becomes a solemn joy. Why should we be pensive and wistful when we think how near our end is? Is the sentry sad as the hour for relieving guard comes nigh? Is the wanderer in far-off lands sad when he turns his face homeward? And why should we not rejoice at the thought that we, strangers and foreigners here, shall soon depart to the true metropolis, the mother-country of our souls? I do not know why a man should be either regretful or afraid as he watches the hungry sea eating away this "bank and shoal of time" upon which he stands—even though the tide has all but reached his feet—if he knows that God's strong hand will be stretched forth to him at the moment when the sand dissolves from under him, and will draw him out of many waters and place him high above the floods in that stable land where there is "no more sea."

Lives rooted in God through faith in Jesus Christ are not vanity. Let us lay hold of Him with a loving grasp—and "we shall live also" *because* He lives, *as* He lives, *so long* as He lives. The brief days of earth will be blessed while they last and fruitful of what shall never pass. We shall have Him with us while we journey—and all our journeyings will lead to rest in Him. True, men walk in a vain show; true, "the world passeth away and the lust thereof"—but, blessed be God! true, also, "He that doeth the will of God abideth forever."

Isaac and Rebekah, Jacob and Rachel— Love, Courtship, Marriage

Clarence Edward Noble Macartney (1879–1957) ministered in Paterson, New Jersey, and Philadelphia, Pennsylvania, before assuming the influential pastorate of First Presbyterian Church, Pittsburgh, Pennsylvania, where he ministered for twenty-seven years. His preaching especially attracted men, not only to the Sunday services but also to his popular Tuesday noon luncheons. He was gifted in dealing with Bible biographies and, in this respect, has been called "the American Alexander Whyte." Much of his preaching was topical-textual, but it was always biblical, doctrinal, and practical. Perhaps his most famous sermon is "Come Before Winter."

The sermon I have selected was taken from *The Way of a Man with a Maid,* published in 1959 by Abingdon Press.

Clarence Edward Noble Macartney

2

ISAAC AND REBEKAH, JACOB AND RACHEL— LOVE, COURTSHIP, MARRIAGE

Wilt thou go with this man? (Genesis 24:58).

And Jacob served seven years for Rachel; and they seemed unto him but a few days, for the love he had to her (Genesis 29:20).

SEPULCHERS AND MARRIAGE altars, burials and betrothals, how close together they come in life! The minister has hardly finished the words of committal, "Dust to dust, earth to earth, ashes to ashes," until he finds himself repeating to the man and the woman the vows of matrimony. So it has been from the beginning. Abraham buried Sarah his wife in the cave of Machpelah and then turned to the business of securing a wife for Isaac. A few pages are turned, and it is Isaac who is being buried and his son, Jacob, who is being married. So it has gone on from the beginning, and so it will go on until the world is lifted to that state where they neither marry nor are given in marriage.

We have here the two most celebrated stories of love, courtship, and marriage in the Old Testament. In the one instance, that of Rebekah and Isaac, marriage came first, and then courtship and love. In the second instance, that of Jacob and Rachel, love and courtship came first, and marriage afterward. But in both instances it was real love, real courtship, and true marriage.

Until time ends, the divine order is what God instituted from the beginning—that a man shall forsake his father and mother and cleave to his wife, and they shall become one flesh. Here in this fundamental fact is the foundation of law, order, human society, the church, and the heavenly

23

commonwealth. Without marriage, all of these are impossible; and they who follow this original institute are helping to carry out the plan and the will of God in the world.

Isaac and Rebekah

This relationship is honored and perpetuated in the marriage service of the Church of England, where the bride and the groom are exhorted to live together "as Isaac and Rebekah lived faithfully together." Sarah had been a model wife and mother to Abram and Isaac, and her death left a great gap in that family circle. Isaac was past forty and not yet married. The reason seems to have been, first of all, a natural and rather attractive diffidence and passiveness of disposition; in the second place, an unusual bond of close affection between this son of the promise and his mother and father. Then there was the fact that they were dwelling in the land of Canaan, which, although the promised land, was a land of idolaters whose inhabitants, unless Abraham was willing to lower his standards, could supply no suitable candidates for the hand of Isaac.

MIXED MARRIAGES

When Abraham is old and well stricken in years, he takes thought for the continuity and succession of his line through Isaac, and plans for his marriage. Some would never take this step unless it were planned for them, and if all could plan as well as Abraham did, there could be little objection to such a manner of procedure. Abraham called his servant, no doubt the faithful Eleazer, who had been over his household for more than half a century, and charged him with an oath to go to Mesopotamia where Abraham's people lived and secure a suitable wife for Isaac. He made him swear to two things. First, that he would not let Isaac take a wife of the people of the land of Canaan, who were idolaters. Second, that he would not let Isaac go back to Mesopotamia, for thence Abraham, faithful to the command of God, had migrated. Therefore, it would not do for his son, to whom the promise was continued, to return to Mesopotamia.

The care which Abraham gave to the marriage of Isaac is to be commended to fathers and mothers today. He charges the one who is to arrange for this marriage that the woman chosen is to be of the same religion, the same race, and the same general family and social standing. Love imagines that it can overleap the barriers of race and blood and religion, and in the enthusiasm and ecstasy of choice these obstacles and barriers appear insignificant. But the facts of experience are against such an idea. Mixed marriages are rarely happy. Observation and experience demonstrate that the marriage of a Gentile and a Jew, a Protestant and a Catholic, an American and a foreigner, has less chance of a happy result than a marriage where the man and the woman are of the same race and religion. Abraham insists that Isaac shall marry a believing woman, and this condition is one which every Christian contemplating marriage should consider. There are not a few who feel that the rite of Christian marriage should be celebrated only when *both* the man and the woman are acknowledged and professed disciples of Christ, and where they undertake to make their home a Christian home and to associate themselves with a Christian church. There is something to be said for that position, for when one is not a professed Christian, the solemn vows made in Christ have little meaning and no binding power.

BY AN ANCIENT WELL

Now the scene shifts to far-off Mesopotamia. With ten camels laden with presents and supplies, the servant of Abraham has reached the city of Nahor. Probably that city was just a collection of adobe huts or scattered tents. But there was one refreshing place in it, and that was the ancient well outside the city. These wells then, and even today, were the meeting place for the people. And here the women gathered, not only to draw water, but to drink the water of social relationship and friendship. Just at the time that the women are coming out to draw water, Eleazer reaches his destination and makes his camels kneel down by the well. When he sees the women approaching with their waterpots upon their shoulders, he asks God to direct him by a sign to the right choice of a wife for Isaac. It is to be noted that this was no insignificant sign, such as people sometimes ask for—a chance meeting, or a number in a series, or a certain color or form of an object—but one which carried with it an index to character. He would ask the first maiden who appeared to let down her pitcher and give him a drink of water. If she responded to his request, and not only gave him water, but volunteered to draw water for his camels, then he would feel satisfied that this was the woman. The sign that he asked for was one which would indicate that the woman who thus responded had a heart of kindness, hospitality, and courtesy—always a pleasing thing in woman.

The prayer of the servant had hardly been finished when Rebekah came out with her pitcher upon her shoulder: "and the damsel was very fair to look upon, a virgin; and she went down to the well and filled her pitcher and came up." As she came up the steps at the mouth of the well, the servant hurried to meet her and said, "Let me, I pray thee, drink a little water of thy pitcher." And Rebekah, with grace and courtesy, responded, "Drink, my lord," at the same time letting down her pitcher and drawing water for him. Then, when she had drawn for him, she volunteered to draw water for his camels. "The man, wondering," the narrative tells us, "held his peace," anxious to know whether the Lord had prospered his journey and if this was to be the woman for Isaac. In silence he watches Rebekah as, with infinite grace in her lithe body and beautiful face, she bows herself to the task of drawing up the water for the thirsty camels, little thinking that at the same time she was weaving the threads of fate and destiny. So ever it is. When we are most self-conscious, our actions may be the least significant. But when we are acting as Rebekah did, spontaneously, naturally, without thought of the results or consequences, we are forging the links in the chain of our destiny.

"Whose daughter art thou?" the man said to Rebekah. When he heard that she was the daughter of Bethuel and

Nahor, and thus a niece of Abraham and a cousin of Isaac, he was overjoyed. Bowing himself down, he worshiped God, saying: "Blessed be the LORD God of my master Abraham, who hath not left destitute my master of his mercy and truth: I being in the way, the LORD led me to the house of my master's brethren."

We do not ask for signs just as this servant did. Yet in the important steps of life and in marriage above all else, because nothing affects one's life so much for better or worse, it is right that we should wait upon God and ask that He would make plain our path. This the servant of Abraham had done all through his long journey. "I *being in the way*," he said, "the LORD led me." People who do not put themselves in the way, or who, in the way, get out of it and follow their own way, need not be surprised if their way leads them astray. With the upright, God has said He will show Himself upright; with the froward He will show Himself froward. If we stay in the way of His commandments, we have a right to expect His blessing and His leadership.

THE GREAT DECISION

Rebekah, with natural grace and hospitality, invites the servant of Abraham to come and lodge in her father's house. In the meantime, her brother, Laban, appears on the scene. He is not yet the hard-boiled Laban of Jacob's romance, but a man of true hospitality and brotherly interest and affection. The camels are unharnessed and given straw and provender for the night, while Eleazer and his companions go to the house of Rebekah. The table is spread with such things as were in the order of hospitality in those days. But this faithful servant knows the psychological moment and says that he will not eat until he has stated his business. Then he rehearses the family history: the birth of Isaac, the death of Sarah, the charge which Abraham gave him, the journey of five hundred miles over the sands, his prayer by the well, and the coming of Rebekah. He then asks point-blank whether or not there is hope for his proposition. If there is not, he will move on to some other collateral branch of

Abraham's family. Laban and Bethuel both answered that the thing seems to be of the Lord, and that if Rebekah is willing to go to be the wife of Isaac, she can go. Then jewels and presents and decorations are brought out of the servant's treasury to deck the beautiful Rebekah and the members of her family.

When morning dawns over the desert—and what were the dreams of Rebekah that night?—the servant is anxious to depart. Laban and Bethuel suggest a wait of ten days. Perhaps they did this so that Rebekah might make more elaborate preparation as to her bridal garments, or perhaps that she might search and know her own mind better. But the wise servant says that now is the accepted time and insists upon an immediate departure. Then the father and brother turn to Rebekah and say those words that have echoed in the world ever since, and in the marriage service, "Wilt thou go with this man?" For her it meant an everlasting farewell to the town where she was born, to her girlhood friends, to the quiet evenings of chatter and gossip by the well. It meant separation from father and mother, brother and sister, if she had any. There was silence for a moment, and then Rebekah made her answer, "I will go." She felt safe in going because the whole subject and matter had been advanced and proposed in the name of God. If the unseen bridegroom was of the same mind as this servant, then she was safe. And yet, after all, as in every such response, it had to be the answer of faith. Rebekah said, "I will go."

How that answer has echoed upon the lips of thousands and thousands of the sisters of Rebekah! "Wilt thou go?" And back has come the answer, "I will go"—no doubt, to those who hear both sentences, earth's sweetest music. "I will go!" and she has gone, although it meant the crossing of broad seas, a hut in a land of savages, a rude frontier settlement, one room in the third story back, which must serve as bedroom, living room, and kitchen. "I will go!" although it has meant separation, loneliness, child-bearing, sickness, grief, sometimes disappointment, sorrow, and tragedy. Yet the world keeps on going because men ask, "Wilt thou go?" and women still answer with radiant eye and tremulous voice, "I will go."

MEDITATION AND THE SOUL

The camels are off again, this time on the great trail to the southwest and the land of Canaan. During those days and nights of travel, Rebekah had plenty of time to think about her journey and her prospective bridegroom. At length they came to the well of Lahai-roi. It was toward the eveningtide, and Isaac had gone out into the fields to meditate. It is then, in that mystic period between the passing of the day and the oncoming of the night, that the mystery and stillness of the world invite thought and meditation. Meditation is the twilight of the soul. It is at the eventide—when all nature whispers of the supernatural, and the temporal seems to reflect the eternal—that doors and windows are opened for us into the heavenly places. That was a promising thing about Isaac. He was not all on the surface. He had moments of introspection and meditation. Before a woman marries a man, it would be well to know whether or not he ever meditates. The same holds true of a man before he marries a woman. On both sides, one ought to know whether with the other it is just a round of activities and pleasures and excitements and moving pictures and comic papers and cheap stories, or whether the soul of the man or the soul of the woman has twilight hours of meditation and of thought. Frivolity in one or both partners to a marriage is, as often as anything else, a source of weariness and distaste on one side or the other. For, as one has said, "A fly is as difficult to tame as a hyena."

The moment Rebekah discerned the form of the contemplating Isaac, with becoming humility and modesty, true to the customs of the East, she alighted from her camel and covered her beauties of face and form with the long veil which then, and even now, prevailed in the East. This veil was a token of modesty, and yet of confidence and intimacy, and has its survival in the veil which the bride wears at the weddings of our own day.

AND HE LOVED HER

It must have been an anxious and critical moment for both Rebekah and Isaac. Suppose that the as-yet-unknown bridegroom should prove repellent to Rebekah? Or what if the bride should be distasteful to Isaac? But this was one of those marriages made in heaven, and the confidence of both Rebekah and Isaac was rewarded by mutual admiration and affection. Isaac dismissed the servant after he had related his story. Her nurse and companion, who thus far had been her chaperon, retired from the black tent. The veil was lifted from her face, and the romance which commenced in Mesopotamia ended in true happiness and true affection. Isaac took her into his mother Sarah's tent, the place sacred to him because of that great mother's memories; "and she became his wife, and he loved her; and Isaac was comforted after his mother's death." So in keeping with the divine plan, how it is not good for the man to be alone, the solitary and mourning Isaac is comforted and companioned by this successor to his mother, who becomes his wife.

Jacob and Rachel

In the story of Jacob and Rachel, we have the way of a man with a maid which is more in keeping with the ideas of our day and generation. Not marriage and then court-ship and love, but love, courtship, and marriage. The marriage service says that Isaac and Rebekah lived faith-fully together, and this is a true record of their relation-ship. The eager, impulsive, affectionate, and daring nature of Rebekah was well adapted to the quiet, medi-tative, and retiring disposition of Isaac.

THE WRONG GIRL

But our last view of the home of Isaac and Rebekah is not an altogether pleasant one. Rebekah, in some strange way, had her strong affections diverted from a natural channel that took in both her sons, Esau and Jacob, to one that embraced Jacob alone. Her whole heart and soul were set on the preferment of Jacob. It is true that, at the birth of these twins, it was told Rebekah that the elder should serve the younger. Moreover, Esau, when he was forty years old, married a woman of the land of Canaan, which was a grief of mind to Isaac, but especially to Rebekah—all credit to her for that. She said: "I am weary of my life because of the daughters of Heth. If Jacob take a wife of the daughters of Heth, what good shall my life do me?" And in that mother's lament and dread we hear the echo of many a mother's voice. Few men marry women who altogether satisfy either their mothers or their sisters, for woman judges woman by herself. It was more of a blow to Rebekah to have Esau take a wife of the daughters of Heth than it would be to a mother today to have a son marry out of his rank and class. The great promises of the future were linked with her offspring, and now that Esau had apostatized, she is doubly anxious to keep Jacob from contamination and to see that he is properly married. The ill-favored plot which she invents and works out for the deception of Isaac so that Jacob gets the blessing of the older son, must be considered in the light of this fact. It was not merely maternal ambition and pride, but religious hopes which animated her.

LOVE AT FIRST SIGHT

Having tricked his brother into selling the birthright and then deceived his father into giving him the blessing which belonged to Esau, Jacob had to flee the country. The first memorable incident on the exile's journey was his wonderful dream at Bethel when he saw a ladder set up on earth, the top of which reached to heaven, and down which and up which went the angels of God. Fortified by this vision, Jacob made his way to what was then the far East, Mesopotamia. One day, far in the distance, Jacob, the lonely fugitive, saw three white dots on the horizon. Being of shepherd folk, he knew that these white dots were three flocks of sheep and that near the sheep there must be a well and a habitation of men. At this his courage revives, and quickening his step he arrives at the well where the three flocks are resting, waiting to be watered. Jacob greets the shepherds as brethren, and he says, "Whence be ye?" They answer, "Of Haran are we." "Know ye Laban, the son of Nahor?" Jacob asked. They answered: "We know him. He is well; and behold, Rachel, his daughter, cometh with the sheep." Jacob turned and looked upon Rachel, and in that glance was contained the whole future history of Jacob and the people of Israel. The Bible, without any mawkishness or apology, frankly recognizes the power and influence of woman's beauty and tells us in the case of both Rebekah and Rachel that they were fair to look upon. So fair was Rachel that with impulsive Jacob it was love at the first sight. As we shall see, not only the first sight, but the second and the third, and on to the very end, until when, but a little way to Ephrath where she had given him the second son, Rachel died and was buried, but never forgotten.

Jacob, inspired by his first glance, ran to the well. Although it was something more than one man's job, because love had multiplied his powers, Jacob himself rolled away the great stone from the well and drew water for the flock of Rachel. That was a good start for Jacob. Chivalry and gallantry at the well won for Moses his bride. At this Mesopotamian well it helped Jacob to win the beautiful Rachel, and by many a well of life the chivalry that comes from the heart and expresses itself in kindness and in courtesy has commended man to woman. Too often this sort of chivalry does not long survive the bridal day and withers under the hot sun of adversity and trial and sickness and daily contact of personalities. But in the case of Jacob, this beautiful chivalry endured to the end. Even the memory of Rachel is sacred to Jacob. This strong man, Jacob, had in him much that was sensual and abominable, together with much that was spiritual and noble. It was fortunate for him that his heart settled on a woman like Rachel.

THE COURSE OF TRUE LOVE

Jacob never did anything in a halfway fashion. He concluded this first act of their drama by kissing Rachel, and thus sealing their affection. Meanwhile, Rachel's father, Laban, came out and invited him into the house. He is not now the generous man whom we saw as a youth and as the brother of Rebekah. He makes a hard bargain with his nephew, Jacob, and practically sells his daughter, Rachel, to Jacob for seven years of hard labor. There was another sister, Leah, not so attractive as the well-favored Rachel, and Jacob had no leanings in that direction. But he was glad to sign an agreement to labor seven years for the hand of Rachel. That would seem a long time to the people of our day and generation, who so often marry in haste and repent at leisure. Long betrothals of this sort ill suit the habits and thoughts of the world today and, perhaps as a rule, are not to be desired. Although, indeed, they do have one advantage— that they afford opportunity for a complete acquaintance and a manifestation of both desirable and not so desirable traits and characteristics.

The course of true love never runs smooth. This saying is as true as it is ancient. Jacob found it to be so. Seven years must have seemed a dreadfully long time to him, and to Rachel, also. Though, no doubt, living in the same encampment, they saw much of one another and took plenty of time to water the sheep at her father's well. Then comes the sentence, which makes this story immortal: "And Jacob served seven years for Rachel, and they seemed to him but a few days for the love he had to her." Ambition, greed, hate—all these will make the day a week, and the week a year. Love is the great reducer and diminisher. So the years passed, and passed as if they were days. This is the kind of love that hopes all things and believes all things and endures all things. Those who have hardship, sickness, poverty, and yet with all this can carry a lantern of mutual love, are to be envied by those who have rank, station, talents, money, comforts, but no love or affection.

RETRIBUTION AND LOVE'S LABOR LOST

At length the seven years are over and the nuptial day so long awaited has arrived. The ceremonies appropriate to the occasion have been finished. Rachel's nurse, like the nurse of Rebekah, conducts her, closely veiled, to the tent of Jacob and retires. The veil is unwound, and lo! it is the face, not of Rachel, but the ill-favored Leah. Jacob's scorn of Leah is easy to understand. What is not so easy to understand at first is the unprotesting manner in which Jacob acquiesces in this disgraceful fraud. Why was this? It must have been the reaction of his own conscience: "Whatsoever evil thing a man doeth, that also shall he receive again." And Jacob was paid in his own coin. He had deceived his own father and cheated his own brother. Now, in the most tender and most sensitive area of his own life, he is cruelly deceived. "Whatsoever a man soweth, that shall he also reap."

We wonder that Jacob did not knock Laban down with his shepherd's staff, gather Rachel in his arms, put her on one of his camels, and elope westward. But the age of elopement had not yet come. So Jacob settled down to another term of service. It is not quite clear from the record whether he actually served another seven years for Rachel, or whether at the end of the week of nuptial celebrations over the marriage with Leah, he was married to Rachel, and then served another seven years. But whether married then or not, he did serve fourteen years for the hand of Rachel and never regretted it. His was the love celebrated in the Song of Songs: "Many waters cannot quench love; neither can the floods drown it. If a man will give all the substance of his house for love, he would utterly be condemned."

HOPE DEFERRED

After the marriage, Rachel, whose cry was, "Give me a child or I die," had to wait for a child almost as long as Jacob had to wait for her. This singular fact, not only in the case of Rachel, but in the case of almost every notable woman in the Scriptures, must have a deep significance. It was so in the case of Sarah; it was so in the case of the mother of Samson; it was so in the case of Hannah, the mother of Samuel; it was so in the case of Rebekah, and of the Shunammite woman; and of Elisabeth, the mother of John the Baptist. What is the meaning of this reiterated record of disappointment and hope deferred? It must be nothing less than to teach us that God wants above all else in His children faith. Faith is life's best child. It also emphasizes the fact that life is a discipline and a probation, even life in its most tender and most intimate relationships.

AND WITH THE MORN THOSE ANGEL FACES SMILE

But at length Rachel's period of waiting was over. First Joseph was born, and then long after, when Jacob had returned to his own country not far from Ephrath, the second son, Benjamin, was born. With this second son, Rachel gave her life and was buried. Jacob set up a pillar upon her grave. He could never forget that day. Long afterward, when he was about to bless the sons of Joseph, the old man can remember the very spot where she died and how far it was from Ephrath, for he says: "When I came from Padan, Rachel died by me in the land of Canaan, in the way, when yet there was yet a little way to come to Ephrath; and I buried her there in the way of Ephrath." Ephrath was Bethlehem, where ages later another mother was to bring forth Jacob's mighty descendant, there Rachel's child was born.

The love of Jacob and his whole life henceforth centered in the two sons of Rachel. When he looked on the face of his youngest son, Benjamin, or when he saw Joseph's coat of many colors flashing in the sunlight, or, on a darker day, all torn and spotted with blood when Joseph's cruel brothers held it up before his father, the one of whom Jacob was thinking was Rachel. When he came to die, Jacob said, "Few and evil have been my days." Life had been full of trouble and sorrow for Jacob. Yet his path had been lighted by the lamp of a wonderful affection. To his dying day Jacob, in the reverie of age, was again a youth in far-off Mesopotamia. Again he saw the three flocks of sheep like snow on the face of the desert; once again by the well he saw the face that was even more wonderful to him than the golden ladder, which in his dream at Bethel he had seen let down from heaven.

The Baby

Clovis Gillham Chappell (1882–1972) was one of
American Methodism's best-known and most effective
preachers. He pastored churches in Washington, D.C.;
Dallas and Houston, Texas; Memphis, Tennessee; and
Birmingham, Alabama; and his pulpit ministry drew
great crowds. He was especially known for his
biographical sermons that made biblical figures live and
speak to our modern day. He published about thirty
volumes of sermons.

This message was taken from *Home Folks,* published
by Abingdon Press.

Clovis Gillham Chappell

3

THE BABY

What manner of child shall this be! (Luke 1:66)

The Fascination of the Baby

Here is a familiar group—a father, a mother, and a company of admiring friends. They are gathered around a cradle. In that cradle is a baby. And these people are looking into the wide eyes of that baby with an interest so keen that you would think that he is the only baby that had ever been born. Of course none had ever been born just like him. And yet such a scene as this has been presented countless millions of times. But in spite of this fact the baby has lost none of its fascination. It is still the most wonderful something that our human eyes have ever seen. Other things may hold our attention for awhile. We may be interested in comets and shooting stars. We may be interested in towering mountains and in seas booming out their thunder upon the rocks. But none of these are to be compared in genuine interest to a real live baby.

One has called attention to Thomas Carlyle, the sage of Scotland, as he is holding a baby in his arms. It is not his own baby. He never had any children of his own. That was his misfortune. He is holding his cousin's baby. And as he holds it he looks into its face with wide-eyed wonder. He seems never to be able to get through marveling at it. "To think," he says, "that Shakespeare was once like this." His delightful interest does not surprise us. There is somehow a fascination about a baby that never grows old.

> Where did you come from, baby dear?
> Out of the everywhere, into the here.
>
> Where did you get those eyes so blue?
> Out of the sky as I came through.

What makes your cheeks like a warm white
   rose?
I saw something fairer than anyone knows.

Whence that three-cornered smile of bliss?
The angels gave me at once their kiss.

And how did you come to us, my dear?
God thought of you and so I am here.

What Is the Secret of This Fascination?

He is a creature of mystery. "What manner of child
shall this be?" Ah, we do not know the answer to that
question. That is one secret of the abiding fascination of
the child. It holds in its chubby hands the lure and charm
of the unknown. It is a bundle of most amazing possibilities. It is a pent-up package of power. Those little
hands may one day sway the rod of empire. Upon those
dimpled feet he may "wade through slaughter to a throne
and shut the gates of mercy on mankind." Those tender
lips may one day be the wide-open gateway through
which God will come to speak a living message to the
hearts of humanity. Poetry may be pent up within him.
A thousand songbirds may be hidden away in his little
baby soul, waiting to burst into melodies that will charm
the coming centuries. He may usher in the dawning of a
new day. Or he may help to lower the moral tempera-
ture of the world. Truly he fascinates us with the mystery of his marvelous possibilities.

A baby is fascinating because of its helplessness. There
is a charm in strength. We all recognize that. We admire
strong things. We are appealed to by the rugged strength
of the oak. We glory in the strength of the athlete. We love
above all else that high moral strength that can brave the
fighting tempests of the world. But we love weakness too.
Weakness gives us a chance to do something that is
Godlike. What is God always doing—morning, noon, and
night? What is He doing from eternity to eternity? He is
helping the weak. He is putting His infinite strength at
the disposal of those who have little strength. He is
undergirding weakness with His everlasting arm. And

when God gives a little child He grants us the high joy of doing something that is Christlike. The baby fascinates us with its clinging, adorable weakness.

Then the baby fascinates us because of its marvelous power. What a mighty something is a baby! Its might is not the might of physical strength. It is the might of love. You can't help loving a baby. And because it is so pure and innocent you cannot but be blessed by that love. I do not believe that any man ever loved a little child who was not made better by that love. The prophet said, "A little child shall lead them." And from generation to generation little children have been leading men out of darkness into light, out of selfishness into unselfishness, out of estrangement and hate into fellowship and love.

What a revolution a little child can work in a human life! It is good to see Little Nell in the "Old Curiosity Shop" become like an angel of light to the hard and unclean man that loves her. It is fine to watch Eppie push the selfishness and hate out of the heart of the miserly weaver of Ravelo, and fill it full of sympathy and love and tenderness. It is fine to see how Cosette redeems her mother from a life of impurity to one of tender self-forgetfulness and sacrifice.

Then there is the charming story in the *Road Mender*. An old organ grinder is one day grinding out his uncouth music in an uncouth street. A little child turns its soiled face up to the hardened face of the old grinder to be kissed. But he is bitter and full of hate. Instead of kissing the child, he strikes her and she runs away weeping. Later he is hurt in an accident and is sent to the hospital. Here he remembers the upturned face of the child and is haunted by it. When he is well again he sets out to find her. He secures the records that children like best. He goes into all the unclean and filthy streets. He never finds her. But as he searches he finds other children, and he finds a new tenderness, a new sympathy, a new heart, a new Savior.

I recall an experience in my own ministry in the city of Forth Worth, Texas. There was a man of my acquaintance that I very much desired to win to Christ. I made more than one effort to have a heart-to-heart talk with him, but always with little success. He was that type of man who is very much afraid of preachers. When I went into his store he had a way of getting frantically busy. He looked as if he were going to wrap up everything in the house. I think if he had had an auto in there he would have made an effort to put a piece of paper around it. Of course I would not interfere with his work while he was so busy. Therefore at every visit I would have to leave without having accomplished my purpose.

But one day I spoke to one of his clerks. I was sure that this clerk knew the man intimately and well. I said to him: "How about our friend? Do you know anything special about him? Has he a hobby? Or has he someone that he peculiarly loves?" And the man thought a moment and then answered: "He has a little girl in his home that he fairly worships." With that important bit of knowledge for my reward I went away.

Some days after that I saw this merchant in my audience. And standing there in my pulpit I talked to him, heart to heart and face-to-face, very largely as if he and I were alone. I talked to him about his little girl. I pleaded with him to give her the best possible chance at life. I urged upon him the importance of throwing around her those Christian influences that make for the best moral support. Then I spoke of the selfishness and the wickedness of allowing her to tangle her innocent feet in his old ragged, selfish, and indifferent life, and fall out into sin in this world and into ruin in the world to come. The man listened intently. And not only did he listen, but he fought his fight and won his victory. And when I stepped into that store a few days later I found him in earnest conversation with one of his clerks. And turning to me he said: "Here is a man who has two little girls in his home, and he is not a Christian. I am trying to win him and want you to help me."

How did this man come to the Cross? He was led there, as so many millions of others have been led, by the mighty and tender hand of a little child. O what a thing of blessed power is a baby! Some of you realize perfectly the truth of what I am saying. You have understood God better since your baby came. And heaven has ceased to be a far-off and unreal place since the little fellow you love slipped away into the miracle country carrying your heart with him.

The Importance of the Baby

"What manner of child shall this be?" This is by far the most important question of this day. It is by far the most important question of any day. I know that a great part of the world does not believe this. I know that a great part of the world has never believed it. That, in large measure, is the secret of the tragic plight of this sin-torn and hate-torn day in which we live. We are paying the penalty in the state and in the church for our neglect of childhood. The baby question is now and must forever remain the most important of all questions.

Of course you may think otherwise. You may think that the most important question is what congress is going to do or what is to be the outcome of the dispute between labor and capital. You may think that the question of supreme importance is how to cure the wave of lawlessness that is sweeping over our land. You may think that our supreme questions concern the doings of armies and navies. But that is where you are mistaken. When you read the newspaper this morning you turned to the first page to find the most important happenings of the day. But you should have turned, as another has said, to that obscure column over toward the back that is headed "Births." Of all the pages of the newspaper, that is ever the most important.

But it seems that we can never be made to believe this. Had you been in a province of the Roman Empire some twenty centuries ago you would have found much to depress you. Some wise men would have said in despair: "Rome's eagles have spread their ugly wings over the wide world, and the beaks of Rome's eagles are sucking the heart blood of the world. The night is upon us, and there is no prospect of dawn." Then suppose you had said: "The outlook is not so despairful as that. The skies are already being tinted with the rosy finger of the dawn. In fact, the 'Dayspring from on high' has already visited us. Over in a stable in the obscure village of Bethlehem a little baby was born last night."

Do you suppose anyone would have believed you? They would have laughed outright and said: "A baby! What is a baby in comparison with Rome? What can a baby's weak hands accomplish in the face of the opposition of the most compactly organized government the world has ever seen?" But in spite of all appearances, that little baby was far mightier than Rome. And since then He has "lifted empires off their hinges and changed the whole course of human history."

You will notice this: that when God wants to move forward He always does so on the feet of little children. When the night had settled grim and dark upon the face of the world, when the Catholic Church had taken our Lord away and had given us a dead ritualism in His stead, God determined to bring back the light. And how did He go about it? He did not send to the world an army of soldiers or of scholars or of philosophers. He stooped down and put a little baby in the arms of an obscure mother in a miner's cottage. And they christened that baby Martin Luther. And thus the darkness fled and there was the dawning of a glad new day.

When religion in England was cold and dead, when the educated were regarding Christianity as an exploded and defeated thing, God determined upon a revival. How did He bring this revival about? He put a baby into the arms of Susanna Wesley. That was all. And that was enough. And it came to pass that that baby rode through the century. As he rode the icicles dropped from the eaves of the houses and the winter-stripped trees put on their verdant foliage, and the birds sang and the flowers bloomed and the human heart stood up in the glad consciousness that God had come.

At this very moment there is an army of invasion marching upon this country of ours. And however we may fortify ourselves, that army is going to conquer. It is going to capture and take possession of absolutely everything that we have. It is going to take possession of every state in the union. It is going to take possession of every city, of every town, of every hamlet. It is going to take possession of every political office. It is going to take possession of every business. It is going to take possession of every school and college and university. It is going to take possession of every church and every home. Nothing is going to be left to us, absolutely nothing.

Who compose this army of invasion? Answer: The children that are in our homes. They are the future conquerors and the future rulers of the world. What they are will determine what the civilization of tomorrow is to be. If there is a larger and better day ahead, it is because we have made these children larger and better men and women than ourselves. It is not to be wondered at, therefore, that our Lord said: "Take heed that you despise not one of these little ones." To despise is to undervalue. Take heed that you do not set a cheap valuation upon the child, for he holds in his baby hands the great tomorrow.

Factors Determining the Future of the Baby

"What manner of child shall this be?" Is there any way of giving an intelligent answer to this question? Is there any method of determining what is to be the character of the child that is now in our homes? In other words, do we live in a world of mere chance or in a world of law? Is the statement of Paul true where he says, "Be not deceived; God is not mocked: for whatsoever a man soweth, that shall he also reap"? We believe that that word is absolutely true. We believe that what a man sows in his field he will reap. We believe also that whatsoever a man sows in the heart of his child, that, too, he will reap.

"What manner of child shall this be?"

That depends in some measure upon the ancestry of the child. Every child has a right to be well born. Some children are "half damned in their birth." There are children who come into the world with poisoned blood in their veins. No man has a right "to sit at the upstairs window of life and pour fiery acid down upon the innocent and unprotected heads of his children." No man has a right to do that which surely tends toward the despoiling of his children that are yet unborn.

Environment has something to do with the answer to this question. It is far harder to grow flowers amidst the unsunned gloom of a back alley than in an unshaded garden in the open country. It is far harder to rear children of sound bodies and clean minds amidst the evils of a slum than in a more wholesome, healthful environment.

But while heredity and environment are of some importance in the answering of this question, by far the most important factor is training. Without the proper training the best ancestry and the most wholesome environment may go for nothing. By proper training both a bad ancestry and a bad environment may be overcome. Therefore, we are safe in saying that the words of the wise man have lost none of their wisdom with the passing of the years: "Train up a child in the way he should go; and when he is old, he will not depart from it."

Now, I wonder if you believe this. It is evident that the Catholics believe it. How is it that their church is waxing stronger and stronger? It is not doing so by the conquests that it makes from without. The Catholics are not half so expert in evangelistic campaigns as we are. They win by this method: When a Catholic man marries a Catholic woman their home becomes a Catholic home. Their children are reared in the Catholic faith.

The Jews believe there is a definite answer to this question. They have been despised and persecuted for long centuries, and yet a Jew is a Jew still around the world. How has this come about? It has not come about by mere chance. It has come about through training. When a Jew marries a Jewess their home is a Jewish home. Their children are reared in the Jewish faith.

Germany believed there was an answer to this question. They believed it was possible for us to determine what manner of child this should be. A few years ago they asked the question as they looked into the face of babyhood. And they said: "This child shall be a soldier." And a soldier the child became. Thus it was that a peace-loving nation was transformed in two generations into one of the greatest warring nations that the world has ever seen.

"What manner of child shall this be?" Is Protestant Christianity to leave the answer to this question to mere chance? Are we willing to hazard the salvation of those we love, are we willing to hazard civilization itself, by a lazy and hazy and indifferent attitude toward this matter of supreme importance? We dare not do so. We must face the fact that the most important work we have on our hands today is the training of our children. Then we must work at our task heartened and made earnest by the following considerations:

A child can become a Christian. He can do so for the simple reason that those characteristics that are essential to entering into the kingdom belong to the child by nature. Take faith, for instance. This is the supreme essential both for finding and pleasing God. Now faith is natural to a child. In fact, he will believe anything you tell him until by deceiving him you teach him to believe otherwise. Were you to tell your child that you climbed up last night and bit a piece out of the face of the moon, he would not ask, "How did you get up there?" He would rather ask, "How did it taste?" It is not surprising, therefore, to hear Jesus saying: "Whosoever shall not receive the kingdom of God as a little child, he shall in no case enter therein."

Not only can a child become a Christian, but he can remain a Christian easier than anybody else. What are some of the difficulties of the adult convert? At times he finds it hard to break away from an evil companionship. At other times he finds it hard to break away from the slavery of evil habits. If he is hindered by none of these, he finds it quite as hard to break away from the habit of Christless and unspiritual thinking.

Not only can a child become a Christian and remain a Christian easier than anybody else, but he makes the best Christian. This statement is perfectly reasonable. Who make the best baseball players? Not those who begin playing at forty. They are those who begin playing in boyhood. Who make the best violinists? Not those who take up the study of music when they are fifty. They are those who begin that study in childhood. Who make the most skilled and effective workers in the church of Jesus Christ? Those who begin that work in their young and tender years.

Not only is it true that a child can become a Christian and remain a Christian easier than anybody else, not only is it true that those coming as children make the most effective Christians; but it is further true that unless they are brought to Christ in childhood, the chances are that they will never become Christians at all. "Can a man be born again when he is old?" He can by the grace of God. But it is a rare miracle, indeed. If our children are not reached for God in their childhood, the chances are that they will never be reached.

We depend almost wholly upon two agencies for the performing of this high task of child training. One is the church and the other is the home. The church is of vast importance, but its opportunity is very limited. It is all but powerless without the home. Therefore, if our children are to be won for Christ, we must not only have wise and Christian training at the hands of pastors and Sunday school teachers, but also at the hands of fathers and mothers. "What manner of child shall this be?" The answer to that question depends mainly upon the kind of training he receives at home. Therefore, by far the most urgent call of this hour is for fathers and mothers who will measure up to their responsibilities to God and to their children by making their homes vitally Christian.

NOTES

The Children's Playground in the City of God

George Campbell Morgan (1863–1945) was the son of a British Baptist preacher and preached his first sermon when he was thirteen years old. He had no formal training for the ministry, but his tireless devotion to the study of the Bible helped him to become one of the leading Bible teachers of his day. Rejected by the Methodists, he was ordained into the Congregational ministry. He was associated with Dwight L. Moody in the Northfield Bible conferences and as an itinerant Bible teacher. He is best known as the pastor of the Westminster Chapel, London (1904–1917 and 1933–1945). During his second term there, he had Dr. D. Martyn Lloyd-Jones as his associate.

Morgan published more than sixty books and booklets, and his sermons are found in *The Westminster Pulpit* (London: Hodder and Stoughton, 1906–1916). This sermon is from volume 1.

George Campbell Morgan

4

THE CHILDREN'S PLAYGROUND IN THE CITY OF GOD

And the streets of the city shall be full of boys and girls playing in the streets thereof (Zechariah 8:5).

One almost expects to hear someone say, "How extremely shocking!" Some people would probably be surprised to know that the Bible says anything about children playing. This verse not only speaks of them playing, but surprises our prejudices by declaring that *boys and girls* are to play together. It even startles us further by saying that boys and girls are to play together *in the streets!* If not inclined to say, "How shocking this is!" I can quite believe that many would say, "Well, it certainly is marvelous." The prophet, inspired of the Spirit of God, knew perfectly well that people would say it was a marvelous thing, so he immediately continued, "Thus saith the LORD of hosts; If it be marvellous in the eyes of the remnant of this people in these days, should it also be marvellous in mine eyes? saith the LORD of hosts." This being put into other words simply means, The thing which surprises you, that you look upon as marvelous, that almost shocks you, is the very thing upon which the heart of God is set. God believes in children playing, He believes in boys and girls playing together, and He believes in them playing in the streets.

This is a picture of the coming age. I do not mind at all what you call it. Call it, if you will, "the golden age." Call it, if you so please, "the millennial age," or if you prefer to drop back into the language of your childhood, speak of it as "the good time coming." It is a picture of the ultimate victory toward which men perpetually looked in the midst of the battle, of the final triumph which was a constant inspiration of earnest and consecrated service. Ever and

49

anon these ancient Hebrew seers saw glimpses of the coming glory, heard notes of the coming harmonies. These men were not near-sighted. They were far-sighted in a far finer sense of that word than that in which we mostly use it today. They saw so far ahead that the things they saw have not yet come to pass. They saw a kingdom established over which a King should rule in righteousness and in equity. They saw a kingdom established in which a King should rule, and—mark well the language—not by the sight of His eyes or by the hearing of His ears. These are the bases of all judgment at the present moment. They very often lead us into error. This coming King is to rule in righteousness and equity, as one who knows perfectly and absolutely all the facts of the case. As these men looked on they saw nature at peace, and in the midst of it a little child at play.

Let us notice the picture which my text suggests. Zechariah speaks of Jerusalem, Zion, the Mountain of the Lord of hosts. This is not a picture of heaven. It is a picture of earth. This is not the picture of a land and conditions beyond the clouds to which men will escape from peril and strife. It is the picture of conditions which are to obtain here in the world where today sinning and sighing and sorrow abound. This is the picture of conditions that will obtain when the prayer that Jesus taught us to pray, and which, alas, we too often pray carelessly, is realized. "Our Father who art in heaven. Hallowed be Thy name. Thy kingdom come. Thy will be done, as in heaven, so on earth." Therefore I say to you that for a glimpse of the kingdom that is to come, I do not come to a Sunday service, but to a Saturday afternoon in a park. When I want to form some true conception of what God's kingdom will be like, I do not go to a prayer meeting but to a playground. I think I have exercised my ministry here long enough for no one to charge me with undervaluing either the prayer meeting or the Sunday service. They are but means to the end, however; that end is the playground for the children. The establishment of the kingdom of God, the building of His city, the healing of all wounds, the realization of all the forces that lie in human life, at their most perfect condition. All that, and more, is by suggestion within my text.

I know there are discrepancies in both, but in the park and the playground you are nearer the Divine ideal for child life. I come there, not because that exhausts the meaning of the coming kingdom, but because it is the only thing like it today. If I come into commercial life, I find there very little like the kingdom of God. In the commercial world "in that day shall there be upon the bells of the horses, HOLY UNTO THE LORD." That is a poetic figure of a great philosophy. If I come into the law courts today I find very little like the kingdom of God. They are doing their best, but it is a very poor best. If I come into the political arena I think I see there men striving after the ideals of the kingdom, yet we are in prison still and hampered by the god of mammon. If I want a glimpse of the kingdom upon which I can base all my interpretation, I haste me to the playground. Be patient with me if I make that personal. If I want my own heart to understand God's coming kingdom, I turn my back upon my study and get to that other room that is as far from the study as I can put it, where all the noise is, and get among my children. There I am nearer to the kingdom than ever I am in my study. Zechariah was a stern prophet who had no soft things to say in the presence of iniquities. Zechariah was a poet who saw the coming glories. Reading his writings up to this point, you can hardly think of him as having time for a child, and yet suddenly, out of his deep heart, illumined by the glory of the coming days, there sings into the ear of all the centuries the most poetic description of the kingdom that I find in the whole of the Old Testament. "The streets of the city shall be full of boys and girls playing in the streets thereof."

I draw your attention, first of all, to what this text reveals as the thought of God for the children. Let us imagine for a moment that we are not in London. We will transport ourselves to that kingdom which is to be, and to that city which the prophet saw. In that city we see, first, that God's ideal for the child is that the child shall play. It is a very significant fact that all the millennial references to the child are references to the child at play. "The sucking child shall play on the hole of the asp, and the weaned child shall put his hand on the basilisk's den." That wonderful day when "the lion shall eat straw like the ox," and the wolf and the lamb shall lie down together in perfect peace, will be the child's playtime. Have you ever taken a child to the zoological gardens, and have you ever been strangely perturbed by the child's deep anxiety to climb over the rails and get in among the polar bears? It is a divine instinct. The child wants to be where God intended it should be and where God means it to be presently, at play with all the lower animals. "A little child shall lead them." It is the child at play, the child in the midst of nature, set there to play.

I charge you that you do not whittle down this word "play" until you have spoiled it. Ruskin says, "Play is an exertion of body or mind made to please ourselves." I think that is a perfectly accurate definition, but I do not think it takes in all the facts of the case. May I suggest that play is work. If you do not believe me and you have a boy four years old, stay at home from business one day. From morning until night do everything that boy does. I very distinctly remember about a year ago, when one of my boys was four years old, he requested me to play horses with him. I agreed to do so on the condition that he be the horse and I the driver. My garden at Norwood runs down in terraces, and I let him go wherever he liked. It is good to let young horses do that. He went to the bottom by one path, turned around and came up again. I had already had enough, but I let him go on. He went down and up that garden six times, and then I said I must go into the house for a few minutes—and I was there an hour.

What is play? Play is work that is not a task set. Play is work, not for profit, but out of pure delight in the exercise of strength. I wish all the young manhood would remember that. Whenever you put gain or profit at the end of play you demoralize the play. The child has no thought of profit in play. It is work, not as a task and not for profit. God's ideal for the child is that it shall play, and the characteristics of a little child at play are merriment, earnestness, pity, defense of the weak. Watch natural and healthy children at play and you will find that all these things are manifest in the midst of the play.

If I may carry this a little further, I would say that God's ideal for the child is that it should play itself into its work. We talk about the kindergarten system as though it were something we had recently discovered, as though we owed it wholly to Froebel. Here it is in Zechariah. He was a long way ahead. We are getting there perhaps sooner than he thought, but there it is— the children at play. If you watch children by careful, loving, tender watching, they will play themselves into the work for which God made them. In this age of collectivist thinking it is good sometimes to reassert the law of the individual. Every individual ought to be able to say concerning his or her life work, "To this end have I been born, and to this end am I come into the world." That is true not merely of the poets, dreamers, and statesmen, but also of the men and women whom we sometimes insult by saying they do mean things. There are no mean things if they come out of the capacity of the man who is doing them.

If a little child learns its work through its play, all through the strenuous years you will find the man playing at his work. I do not mean playing with his work or doing it indifferently, but that it will be a delight to him. When work is what it ought to be in human life it is not a task set, not something done for profit merely, but something done for the sake of the thing done. I have been in a carpenter's shop and seen a man at the bench making some plain piece of furniture, and looking at it and touching it with love as he saw it developing under his hand. That is the real carpenter, brother to Jesus of Nazareth. If you find a man who loves his work he will have as secondary motive under it all the two things for which Paul says we are to work, the support of himself and his family, and to have something to give to him that is in need. Beyond that, work is done for the sake of the work, but children never come to that unless you give them their chance to play. You must begin with playtime for the children. That is God's ideal.

Then notice, further, that there is in the text a revelation of the fact that it is God's purpose that boys and girls shall play together. I can quite imagine that some very good people out of this age, if they could be preserved until that day dawns and came to this city and saw boys and girls playing together, would think everything had gone wrong, that some catastrophe had happened. I walk around among our schools today and I see over one door "Boys," a little further on I find another door marked "Girls." Presently I come to the "Young Men's Christian Association," and a little farther on I see the "Young Women's Christian Association." We have been doing all we can to keep them apart. We are all wrong. God said boys and girls are to play together. Wherever you find that they do so, naturally, purely, perfectly, you will find that the strength of manhood strengthens womanhood, and the refinement of womanhood refines manhood. That is the perfect family in which brothers and sisters grow up and play together. That is God's ideal. The streets of God's city shall be full of boys and girls playing in the streets thereof.

If that be so, we may go yet a step further, and upon this foundation truth of God's purpose for the child and God's ideal for the child build the conditions of public life. This text is an index to the conditions of public life in the coming kingdom. If in God's city boys and girls are to play in the streets of the city, then the streets of the city will be fit for the boys and girls to play in. Think what that means in the very simplest way. As Christ makes the child the type of character in His kingdom, so the child comes to be the test of public life in the city of God. Everything in the life of the coming city will depend upon the little child. Everything will be carried forward in the interests of the little child. Among other things, the streets will be fit for children to play in. Said Isaiah, another of these prophets, "They shall not hurt nor destroy in all My holy mountain." What a city that will be where there will be nothing in the streets to harm little children—physically, mentally, or spiritually! When you have a city with streets fit for children, you have a city with streets fit for adults. If the child is safe, everyone is safe. Let us walk in imagination through some of the streets of the city of the King. I shall find nothing that can harm the child physically. In that city the drainage will be perfect, and the traffic and everything else will be watched by vigilant eyes for the sake of the children. You can dream your dreams around that. You tell me this is not the Gospel. Then what in the name of God is it? These children whom God loves and speaks of in the terms of playtime in His coming city are to be safe. The measure in which children are safe in our streets today is the measure in which we have seen this ideal and are working toward it.

As we walk through the streets of the city of the King, I notice in the next place that in no single shop window can I find any impure literature. On no placard station can I see a bill announcing an amusement, the very bill suggestive of evil and calculated to inflame the passion of a child or youth. No unholy picture can be found. The love of the child will be greater than love of gain. That is the truth about the city of God.

As I go through these streets of the city I find no man ready to pollute young life. There is no man standing in the shadow of the sanctuary or of the public house watching for his chance to lead a boy who is hardly a youth into the ways of betting and gambling. By no means. In the city of the King the dictum of Jesus will be in operation. The man who is found causing a little child to offend will have a millstone hung about his neck and be drowned in the depth of the sea while angels rejoice. There will be nothing anemic and sickly in the city of the King. Righteous wrath will be manifested if anything is done to offend, or cause to stumble, one little child. The streets of the city are to be fit for the children.

Let us go one step further. It seems to me that my text not only reveals to me the purpose and thought of God for children, not only reveals to me what the conditions of public life are to be in the city, but it casts its light upon the home life in the coming kingdom. It is not only true that the streets are to be fit for the children, but equally true that the children are to be fit for the streets. There are children who come from very respectable houses who pollute the streets by their presence. There are children—proud, despotic, selfish, and, alas, too often impure—to turn whom out to play in the streets would be to defile the other children. I am not blaming the children, for wherever you find such children the blame must be put back on the home from which they come. A child always reflects the home from which it has come.

That legend which you hang up in your homes, "Christ is the Head of this house, the unseen Guest at every meal, the silent Listener to every conversation," will be a living reality in that kingdom. In homes where these things are believed and acted upon from break of day until the sun has gone westering, you will have children that you may turn out into the streets who will not harm the streets or pollute them. In the city of the King the home life will be what it ought to be. Out of the homes will come children whose obedience has been won, whose trust has been inspired, to whom high ideals have been presented, not so much by precept as by the practice of those who have had charge of them. Out of the homes will come children who know God because they have seen Him in the fatherhood and motherhood that has been round about them. Coming out into the streets they will live and walk in the power of all that home has meant to them—children fit for the streets.

If there is one thing tragic in this city, it is the picture of the children who have no playtime. What you call their playtime is for some of them opportunity for deeper debasement. Why? Because our streets are not fit for the children. Because we have never yet put a little child in the midst of us in our civic affairs and set everything else around the necessity of the little child. I am perfectly well aware that we are struggling toward it, but it is so slow because we have never seen it clearly. Sometimes one's heart is gladdened spiritually, religiously, by things that seem to be very far away and yet are near to the heart of God.

I remember seeing awhile ago what came to me as a vision of God's coming glory. I was at the very end of Cheapside, close to the Bank and the Exchange. Suddenly I saw a policeman, a great, strong, muscular representative of the force of the law, raise his hand and hold up all the beating, surging traffic to take a wee bit child by the hand and lead it safely across the street. By so much as we have learned to do that we are coming nearer to the kingdom. But, oh, my masters, how much there is still to harm the life of the child in our streets. You who listen to me tonight dare not turn your children into the streets to play, but there are children playing in the streets who have no other place to play in. In the hearts of all children there is capacity for good and the love of the beautiful just as much as in the hearts of your children, if you will find it.

I will tell you a story at second hand. A month or two ago the first Minister of Works of the present Government was walking in St. James's Park. Two or three children were playing there, one of them a girl with tousled hair, dirty and unkempt. The Minister of Works looked down at this child and said, "Why do you stay here? Why don't you go over there into the Green Park where you can play on the grass?" The bright eyes looked up into his, and she said, "There are no flowers there." Oh, if we could hear these things! I am not arguing for flowers over there, or if I do argue for them it is that they may gladden the children.

Let us see deeply into this thing. You and I have a responsibility about our streets for the sake of the children. You care nothing for political parties? So much the better. You care nothing about Moderates or Progressives or Municipal Reform? So much the better; but do you care for the children? I have figures and statistics that we have been gathering, for we are trying to find out what we ought to do. Do you know such things as this? Right here under the shadow of this church—I begin there for this is our responsibility—there are at least 132 houses in which, on an average, three or four families are crowded together. These children must come out into the streets to play, and the streets are not fit for them. The homes from which they come are not homes that make it likely that their coming will be a blessing to the streets. Are you content to say you have nothing to do with all these things? Say at once you have nothing to do with the kingdom of God. Say at once you have no interest in the bringing in of that great and glad golden age toward which seers have been looking and of which psalmists have been singing. You like to look on to that great day and to sing of it. But I think that the men and women who have not shared the travail that makes His kingdom come are very likely to be shut out of the kingdom when it does come. I want to lay upon you the burden of this great and terrible responsibility.

I am told there is nothing we can do, or that what we can do is so little. You are not responsible for all that has to be done. You are responsible for the thing that lies next to your hand. You are responsible, first of all, to see to it that whatever you have of influence, whatever you may have of influence, whatever lies at your disposal by way of influence, you ought to take hold of and use in the interest of, I will not say the kingdom of God as a far distant thing, but of the little child in the streets. What about the children who are not orphans but are worse than orphans? What about the children who are in sorrow and sore need round about us in our own parish? In our parish there are thirty-four public houses, every last one of them a center of death, an instrument for spoiling childhood. There are portions of these streets of Westminster close to us which are nameless as to their condition. You put the blame upon the police. I put the blame finally upon the church of Jesus Christ.

These men of old, these prophets, how they toiled and strove, how they entered into every department of human life with their messages, their fire, their inspiration, their daring, their suffering, and their blood. What matters it that they never saw the city, if they saw it from afar? They set their faces toward it and died in faith, not having received the promises. Yet the promises would be much longer postponed if they had not so suffered and toiled, and had not so striven. So I say we are working, not merely for the present hour, but for all the future. We are working with the little child before our eyes, determined as the moments come and go to strive and toil and suffer to make the streets fit for the children. We are working to see to it that they have homes out of which it is possible for them to come with some suspicion at least of what morality, cleanness, and uprightness really mean. There is no child in all this crowded district that is not as near to the heart of God as the little child you laid to rest in its cot at home. There is no boy who is not protected from the rain and hardly dare go home, and who will become a sharper on the street, robbing you on every hand—there is not one such who is not referred to by Jesus when He said, "It is not the will of your Father who is in heaven, that one of these little ones should perish."

I say to you tonight that our responsibility as a church and as Christian people for this district must begin there. I am not saying all that is in my heart. I am not saying all I know, but I am making an appeal to you for your interest in prayer, and presently in very definite work. Under the shadow of this church close at hand stands a man day after day, a bookmaker. He has been fined again and again. He pays a fine as I pay a license to keep a dog. Yet he comes back and carries on his nefarious practices. I am told that we must let these things alone. My answer is that the Devil said to Jesus, "Let us alone." Christ's answer is our answer to all these things. We will not let it alone. It is our business not to let it alone. A way must be found by which these men shall be removed and it be made impossible for them to stand around luring our children to destruction. It is very little we can do. In a few years at least the majority of us will have gone out to the great beyond, but let us do something. Let us, at any rate, come to close grips with the Devil. Let us leave the impress of our fingers somewhere on him or else let us be ashamed to look into the face of Jesus

Christ when the day breaks and the shadows flee away.

Our city is not the city Zechariah saw. The streets of our city are not ready for the boys and girls to play in. It is our business as we take our way through this life of probation and toil and discipline to see the ultimate and to consecrate ourselves to that great and holy conflict which at last is to issue in victory. I pray that we may make what application of the study of this verse is necessary for our own new inspiration to new consecration to the thing that lies very near at hand.

"Where shall I begin?" says some man. In your own home. "How shall I begin?" Set the millennium up in your own home. "How can I do it?" Crown Christ there. I do not mean theoretically, sentimentally. I do not mean by singing about Him or praying to Him or reading the things He said. But do it by the realization of His ideal there for your own children and by realization of His ideal in your home as Master and Lord and King. Every home so consecrated and so realizing His ideal is a contribution toward the building of God's city. We may begin there, and yet to begin and end there is not to fulfill our responsibility. We must go beyond and what we cannot do singly we must do together. As the host of God we must say to the civic authorities and to all the powers that rule the city's life, "These rulings and governings of yours must be in the interest of the child." If that can be established then I have no further care about the youth and maiden, man and woman, about the aged and infirm. We will begin with the child. God help us to hear His call to us about this district through the plaintive need of the child as it expresses itself to all who have eyes to see, and ears to hear, and hearts to feel.

NOTES

The Young Man's Prayer

Charles Haddon Spurgeon (1834–1892) is undoubtedly the most famous minister of the nineteenth century. Converted in 1850, he united with the Baptists and soon began to preach in various places. He became pastor of the Baptist church in Waterbeach, England, in 1851, and three years later he was called to the decaying Park Street Church, London. Within a short time the work began to prosper, a new church was built and dedicated in 1861, and Spurgeon became London's most popular preacher. In 1855, he began to publish his sermons weekly; today they make up the fifty-seven volumes of *The Metropolitan Tabernacle Pulpit*. He founded a pastor's college and several orphanages.

This sermon was taken from *The Metropolitan Tabernacle Pulpit,* volume 9.

Charles Haddon Spurgeon

5

THE YOUNG MAN'S PRAYER

O satisfy us early with thy mercy; that we may rejoice
and be glad all our days (Psalm 90:14).

ISRAEL HAD SUFFERED a long night of affliction. Dense was
the darkness while they abode in Egypt, and cheerless
was the glimmering twilight of that wilderness which
was covered with their graves. Amidst a thousand
miracles of mercy, what must have been the sorrows of
a camp in which every halt was marked with many
burials until the whole track was a long cemetery? I
suppose that the mortality in the camp of Israel was
never less than fifty each day—if not three times that
number—so that they learned experimentally that verse
of the psalm, "For we are consumed by thine anger, and
by thy wrath are we troubled." Theirs was the weary
march of men who wander about in search of tombs. They
traveled toward a land which they could never reach,
weary with a work the result of which only their children
should receive. You may easily understand how these
troubled ones longed for the time when the true day of
Israel should dawn, when the black midnight of Egypt
and the dark twilight of the wilderness should both give
way to the rising sun of the settled rest in Canaan. Most
fitly was the prayer offered by Moses—the representative
man of all that host—"O satisfy us early with thy mercy."
Hasten the time when we shall come to our promised
rest. Bring on speedily the season when we shall sit
under our own vine and our own fig tree "and shall rejoice
and be glad all our days."

This prayer falls from the lips of yonder brother, whose
rough pathway for many a mile has descended into the
Valley of Deathshade. Loss after loss has he experienced,
until as in Job's case, the messengers of evil have trodden

upon one another's heels. His griefs are new every morning and his trials fresh every evening. Friends forsake him and prove to be deceitful brooks. God breaks him with a tempest. He finds no pause in the ceaseless shower of his troubles. Nevertheless, his hope is not extinguished, and his constant faith lays hold upon the promise that "weeping may endure for a night, but joy cometh in the morning." He understands that God will not always chide, neither does He keep His anger forever. Therefore he watches for deliverance even as they that watch for the morning. His most appropriate cry is, "O satisfy us early with Your mercy. Lift up the light of Your countenance upon us, show Your marvelous loving-kindness in this present hour of need. O my God, make haste to help me, be a very present help in time of trouble. Fly to my relief lest I perish from the land. Awake, for my rescue, that I may rejoice and be glad all my days."

See yonder sickbed! Tread lightly, lest perchance you disturb the brief slumbers of that daughter of affliction. She has tossed to and fro days and nights without number, counting her minutes by her pains and numbering her hours with the paroxysms of her agony. From that couch of suffering where many diseases have conspired to torment the frail body of this child of woe, where the soul itself has grown weary of life and longs for the wings of a dove, I think this prayer may well arise: "O satisfy us early with thy mercy." "When will the eternal day break upon my long night? When will the shadows flee away? Sweet Sun of Glory! when will You rise with healing beneath Your wings? I shall be satisfied when I wake up in Your likeness, O Lord. Hasten that joyful hour. Give me a speedy deliverance from my bed of weakness that I may rejoice and be glad throughout eternal days."

I think the prayer would be equally appropriate from many a distressed conscience where conviction of sin has rolled heavily over the soul, until the bones are sore vexed and the spirit is overwhelmed. That poor heart indulges the hope that Jesus Christ will one day comfort it and become its salvation. It has a humble hope that these woundings will not last forever, but shall all be healed by mercy's hand. It has a humble hope that he who loosens the bands of Orion will one day deliver the prisoner out of his captivity. Oh! conscience-stricken sinner, you may on your knees now cry out, "O satisfy me early with Your mercy. Keep me not always in this house of bondage. Let me not plunge forever in this slough of despond. Set my feet upon a rock and wash me from my iniquities. Clothe me with garments of salvation, and put the new song into my mouth that I may rejoice and be glad all my days."

Still it appears to me that, without straining so much as one word even in the slightest degree, I may take my text this morning as the prayer of a young heart expressing its desire for present salvation. To you, young men and women, shall I address myself. May the good Spirit cause you in the days of your youth to remember your Creator. While the evil days come not nor the years draw near, when you shall say we have no pleasure in them, I hope the angel of the Lord has said to me, "Run, speak to that young man." And that like the good housewife in the Proverbs, I shall have a portion also for the women!

I shall use the text in two ways: first, *as the ground work of my address to the young*; then, secondly, *as a model for your address to God.*

The Ground Work of My Address to the Young

We will make our text the ground work of a solemn pleading with young men and women to give their hearts to Christ this day. The voice of wisdom reminds you in this our text that you are not pure in God's sight, but need His mercy. Early as it is with you, you must come before God on the same footing as those who seek Him at the eleventh hour. Here is nothing said about merit, nothing concerning the natural innocence of youth, and the beauty of the juvenile character. You are not thus flattered and deceived. But Holy Scripture guides you aright by dictating to you an evangelical prayer such as God will deign to accept: "O satisfy us early *with thy mercy*." Young man, though as yet no outward crimes have stained your character, yet your salvation must be the work of reigning grace, and that for several reasons. *Your nature is at the present moment full of sin and saturated with iniquity.* Hence, you are the object of God's most righteous anger. How can He meet an heir of wrath on terms of justice? His holiness cannot endure you. What if you be made an heir of glory, will not this be grace and grace alone? If ever you are made meet to be a partaker with the saints in light, this must surely be love's own work. Inasmuch as your nature, altogether apart from your actions, deserves God's reprobation, it is mercy which spares you. If the Lord be pleased to renew your heart, it will be to the praise of the glory of His grace. Be not proud—repel not this certain truth—that you are an alien, a stranger, an enemy born in sin and shapen in iniquity, by nature an heir of wrath, even as others. Yield to its force and seek that mercy, which is as really needed by you as by the hoary-headed villain who rots into his grave, festering with debauchery and lust.

> True you are young, but there's a stone
>   Within the youngest breast;
> Or half the crimes which you have done
>   Would rob you of your rest.

Besides, your conscience reminds you that your outward lives *have not been what they should be.* How soon did we begin to sin! While we were yet little children we went astray from the womb, speaking lies. How rebellious we were! How we chose our own will and way and would by no means submit ourselves to our parents! How in our riper youth we thought it sport to scatter fire-brands and carry the hot coals of sin in our bosom. We played with the serpent, charmed with its azure scales, but forgetful of its poisoned fangs. Far be it from us to boast with the Pharisee, "Lord, I thank thee that I am not as others." But rather let the youngest pray with the publican, "God be merciful to me a sinner." A little child, but seven years of age, cried when under conviction of sin, "Can the Lord have mercy upon such a great sinner as I am, who has lived seven years without fearing and loving Him?" Ah!

my friends, if this babe could thus lament, what should be the repentance of those who are fifteen, or sixteen, or seventeen, or eighteen, or twenty, or who have passed the year of manhood. What shall you say since you have lived so long wasting your precious days—more priceless than pearls—neglecting those golden years, despising divine things, and continuing in rebellion against God? Lord, You know that young though we be, we have multitudes of sins to confess. Therefore it is mercy, mercy, mercy, that we crave at Your hands.

Remember, beloved young friends, that if you be saved in the morning of life, *you will be wonderful instances of preventing mercy*. It is great mercy which blots out sin. But who shall say that it is not equally great mercy which prevents it? To bring home yonder sheep—which has long gone astray, with its wool all torn, its flesh bleeding, and its bones broken—manifests the tender care of the good Shepherd. But, oh! to reclaim the lamb at the commencement of its strayings, to put it into the fold, and to keep it there and nurture it. What a million mercies are here compressed into one! The young saint may sweetly sing—

> I still had wander'd but for thee;
> Lord, 'twas thine own all-powerful word,
> Sin's fetters broke, and set me free,
> Henceforth to own thee as my Lord.

To pluck the sere brand from out of the fire when it is black and scorched with the flame, there are depths of mercy here. But are there not heights of love when the young wood is planted in the courts of the Lord and made to flourish as a cedar? However soon we are saved, the glory of perfection has departed from us. But how happy is he who tarries but a few years in a state of nature, as if the fall and the rising again walked hand in hand. No soul is without spot or wrinkle, but some stains are spots the young believer is delivered from happily. Habits of vice and continuance in crime he has not known. He never knew the drunkard's raging thirst. The black oath of the swearer never cancered his mouth. This younger

son has not been long in the far country; he comes back
before he has long fed the swine. He has been black in
the sight of God. But in the eyes of men and in the open
vision of onlookers, the young believer seems as if he had
never gone astray. Here is great mercy, mercy for which
heaven is to be praised forever and ever.

This, I think, I may call *distinguishing* grace with an
emphasis. All election distinguishes, and all grace is discriminating. But that grace, which adopts the young
child so early, is distinguishing in the highest degree. As
Jenubath, the young son of Hadad, was brought up in
the court of Pharaoh and weaned in the king's palace,
so are some saints sanctified from the womb. Happy is
it for any young man, an elect one out of the elect is he,
if he be weaned upon the knees of piety and dandled upon
the lap of holiness, if he be lighted to his bed with the
lamps of the sanctuary and lulled to his sleep with the
name of Jesus! If I may breathe a prayer in public for
my children, let them be clothed with a little ephod like
young Samuel and nourished in the chambers of the
temple like the young prince Joash. O my dear young
friends, it is mercy, mercy in a distinguishing and peculiar degree, to be saved early because of your fallen nature, because of sin committed, and yet more because of
sin prevented and distinguishing favor bestowed.

But I have another reason for endeavoring to plead with
the young this morning, hoping that the Spirit of God will
plead with them. I remark that salvation, if it comes to
you, must not only be mercy, *but it must be mercy through
the Cross.* I infer that from the text, because the text desires it to be a satisfying mercy, and there is no mercy
which ever can satisfy a sinner but mercy through the
cross of Christ. Many preach a mercy apart from the Cross.
Many say that God is merciful and, therefore, surely He
will not condemn them. But in the pangs of death and in
the terrors of conscience, the uncovenanted mercy of God
is no solace to the soul. Some proclaim a mercy that is dependent upon human effort, human goodness, or human
merit, but no soul ever yet did or could find any lasting
satisfaction in this delusion. Mercy by mere ceremonies,

mercy by outward ordinances is but a mockery of human thirst. Like Tantalus, who is mocked by the receding waters, so is the ceremonialist who tries to drink where he finds all comfort flying from him.

Young man, the cross of Christ has in it that which can give you solid, satisfying comfort if you put your trust in it. It can satisfy *your judgment*. What more logical than the great doctrine of substitution? God so terribly just that He will by no means spare the guilty, and that justice wholly met by Him who stood in the room, place, and stead of His people! Here is that which will satisfy your *conscience*. Your conscience knows that God must punish you. It is one of those truths which God stamped upon it when He first made you what you are. But when your soul sees Christ punished instead of you, it pillows its head right softly. There is no resting place for conscience but at the Cross. Priests may preach what they will, and philosophers may imagine what they please, but there is in the conscience of man, in its unrestingness, an indication that the cross of Christ must have come from God. Conscience never ceases from its disquiet until it hides in the wounds of the Crucified. Never again shall conscience alarm you with dreadful thoughts of the wrath to come if you lay hold of that mercy, which is revealed in Jesus Christ.

Here, too, is satisfaction *for all your fears*. Do they pursue you today like a pack of hungry dogs in full pursuit of the stag? Fly to Christ and your fears have vanished! What has that man to fear for whom Jesus died? Need he alarm himself when Christ stands in his stead before the eternal throne and pleads there for him? Here, too, is satisfaction *for your hopes*. He that gets Christ gets all the future wrapped up in Him. While

> There's pardon for transgressions past;
> It matters not how black their cast . . .

There are also peace and joy and safety for all the years and for all the eternity to come in the same Christ Jesus who has put away your sin. Oh! I wish young man, I wish young woman, that you would put your trust in

Jesus now, for in Him there is an answer to this prayer: "O satisfy us early with thy mercy."

Furthermore, anxiously would I press this matter of a youthful faith upon you, *because you have a dissatisfaction even now*. Do I not speak the truth when, looking into the bright eyes of the most cheerful among you, I venture to say that you are not perfectly satisfied. You feel that something is lacking. My lad, your boyish games cannot quite satisfy you. There is something in you more noble than toys and games can gratify. Young man, your pursuits of business furnish you with some considerable interest and amusement, but still there is an aching void—you know there is. Although pleasure promises to fill it, you have begun already to discover that you have a thirst that is not to be quenched with water and a hunger that is not to be satisfied with bread. You know it is so.

The other evening when you were quite alone, when you were quietly thinking matters over, you felt that this present world was not enough for you. The majesty of a mysterious longing that God had put in you lifted up itself and claimed to be heard! Did it not? The other day, after the party was over at which you had so enjoyed yourself, when it was all done and everybody was gone and you were quite quiet, did you not feel that even if you had these things every day of your life, yet you could not be content? You want you know not what, but something you do want to fill your heart. We look back upon our younger days and think that they were far happier than our present state. We sometimes fancy that we used to be satisfied then, but I believe that our thoughts imagine a great falsehood.

I do from my soul confess that I never was satisfied until I came to Christ. When I was yet a child I had far more wretchedness than ever I have now. I will even add more weariness, more care, more heartache than I know at this day. I may be singular in this confession, but I make it and know it to be the truth. Since that dear hour when my soul cast itself on Jesus, I have found solid joy and peace. But before that all those supposed merriments of early youth, all the imagined ease and joy of boyhood, were but vanity and vexation of spirit to me.

You do feel, if I know anything about you, that you are not quite satisfied now. Well, then, let me say to you again that I would have you come to Jesus, for depend upon it there is in Him that which can thoroughly satisfy you. What can you want more to satisfy *your heart* than love to Him? Our hearts all crave for an object upon which they may be set. We often surrender ourselves to an unworthy object that betrays us or proves too narrow to accommodate our heart's desire. But if you love Jesus you will love one who deserves your warmest affection, who will amply repay your fullest confidence, and will never betray it.

You say that not only does your heart want something, but your *head*. My witness is that there is in the Gospel of Christ the richest food for the brain. Before you know Christ you read, you search, you study, and you put what you learn into a wild chaos of useless confusion. But after you have found Christ, everything else that you learn is put in its proper place. You get Christ as the central sun, and then every science and fact begins to revolve around Him, just as the planets travel in their perpetual circle around the central orb. Without Christ we are ignorant, but with Him we understand the most excellent of sciences, and all others shall fall into their proper place.

This is an age when, without a true faith in Christ, the young mind has a dreary pilgrimage before it. False guides are standing, arrayed in all sorts of garbs, ready to lead you first to doubt this book of Scripture, then to distrust the whole, then to mistrust God and Christ, and then to doubt your own existence. They stand ready to bring you into the dreary dreamland where nothing is certain, but where everything is myth and fiction. Give your heart to Christ, young man, and He will furnish you with anchors and good anchor-hold to your mind so that when stormy winds of skepticism sweep across the sea and other barks are wrecked, you shall outride the storm and shall evermore be safe.

It is a strange thing that people should be so long before they are satisfied. Look at some of my hearers today. They mean to be satisfied with money. When they were apprentices they thought they should be so satisfied when they earned journeymen's wages. But they came to be journeymen, and then they were not satisfied until they were foremen. Then they felt they never should be satisfied until they had a concern of their own. They got a concern of their own and took a house in the city. But then they felt they could not be content until they had taken the adjoining premises. Then they had more advertising and more work to do, and now they begin to feel that they never shall be quite easy until they have purchased a snug little villa in the country. Yes, there are some here who have the villa, and handsome grounds, and so on. But they will not be satisfied until they see all their children married. When they have seen all their children married, they will not be at rest then. They think they will, but they will not. There is always a something yet beyond. "Man never is, but always to be blessed," as Young puts it. There are fortunate isles for the mariner to reach, and failing these there is no haven for him even in the safest port.

We know some, too, who, instead of pursuing wealth, are looking after fame. They have been honored for that clever piece of writing, but they are emulous of more honor. They must write better still. When they have achieved some degree of notoriety through a second attempt, they will feel that now they have a name to keep up. They must have that name widened, and the circle of their influence must extend. The fact is, that neither wealth, nor honor, nor anything that is of mortal birth can ever fill the insatiable, immortal soul of man. The heart of man has an everlasting hunger given to it, and if you could put worlds into its mouth it would still crave for more. It is so thirsty that if all the rivers drained themselves into it, still, like the deep sea that is never full, the heart would yet cry out for more. Man is truly like the horse-leech, ever he says, "Give! give! give!" Until the Cross be given to the insatiable heart, until Jesus

Christ, who is the fullness of Him that fills all in all, be bestowed, the heart of man never can be full.

Where shall we find a satisfied man but in the church of Christ? And in the church of Christ I find him, not in the pulpit merely where success and position might satisfy, but I find him in the pew humbly receiving the truth. I find him in the pew, not among the rich where earthly comforts might tend to make him satisfied, but among the poor where cold and nakedness might cause him to complain. I could point you today to the workman who earns every bit of bread he eats with more sweat of his brow than you would dream of, but he is content. I could point you to the poor working girl who scarcely earns enough to hold body and soul together, and yet in this house of God her heart often leaps for joy, for she is wholly resigned. I could show you the bedridden woman whose bones come through the skin through long lying upon a bed, which friendship would fain make soft, but which is all too hard for her weakness. Yet she is content, though a parish pittance be all that is given her to feed upon. I say we have no need to exaggerate or strain or use hyperboles. We do find in the church of Christ those who have been and still are satisfied with the mercy of God.

Now, would it not be a fine thing to begin life with being satisfied? There are some who do not end it with this attainment. They hunt after satisfaction until they come to their dying beds and then do not find it at last. But oh! to begin life with being satisfied! Not to say at some future date I will be satisfied, but to be content now. Not when I have climbed to such-and-such a pinnacle I shall have enough, but to have enough now, to begin with satisfaction before you launch upon a world of troubles! You may do so, my brother; you may do so, my young sister, if now with a true heart you look to Him who hangs upon yonder cross and commit your soul into His keeping, praying this prayer—"O satisfy us *early* with thy mercy."

The reason, which our text gives, I must comment upon for a moment. Our text says, "O satisfy us early with thy mercy; *that we may rejoice and be glad all our days.*" We never rejoice in the true sense of the term. We never possess solid gladness until we are satisfied with God's mercy. It is all a mockery and a pretense. The reality never comes to us until God's mercy visits our hearts. But after that what joy we know! Tell me that the Christian is miserable! O sir, you do not know what the Christian is. We need not appear before you with laughing faces, for our joy is deeper than yours and needs not to tell itself out in immodest signs. The poor trader puts all his goods in the window, but the rich man has rich stores even in the dark cellar. His warehouses are full, and he makes no show. Still waters run deep, and we are sometimes still in our joy because of the depth of our delight.

Say we are not happy! Sirs, we would not change one moment of our joy for a hundred years of yours! We hear your joy and understand that it is like the crackling of thorns under a pot, which crackle all the louder because they burn so furiously and will so soon be gone. But ours is a steady fire. We do mourn sometimes; we mourn more often than we ought to do. We are free to confess this, but it is not our religion that makes us mourn. It is because we do not live up to it, for when we live up to it and have the company of Jesus, we tell you

> We would not change our blest estate
> For all that earth calls good or great;
> And while our faith can keep her hold,
> We envy not the sinner's gold.

Our sick-beds are often as the doorstep of heaven. Even when we are cast down, there is a sweet solace in our sorrow and a profound joy about our apparent grief that we would not give away. God gave it to us, and the world cannot destroy it. They who love Jesus Christ early have the best hope of enjoying the happiest days as Christians. *They will have the most service,* and the service of God is perfect delight. Their youthful vigor will enable them to do more than those who enlist when they are old and decrepit. The joy of the Lord is our strength; on the other hand, to use our strength for God is a fountain of joy.

Young man, if thou give fifty years of service to God, surely you shall rejoice all your days. The earlier we are converted, having the longer time to study in Christ's college, *the more profound shall be our knowledge of Him.* We shall have more time for communion, more years for fellowship. We shall have more seasons to prove the power of prayer and more opportunities to test the fidelity of God than we should if we came late. Those who come late are blessed by being helped to learn so much, but those that come in early shall surely outstrip them. Let me be young, like John, that I may have years of loving service and like him may have much of intimate acquaintance with my Lord.

Surely those who are converted early may reckon upon more joy because *they never will have to contend with and to mourn over what later converts must know.* Your bones are not broken. You can run without weariness. You have not fallen as some have done; you can walk without fainting. Often the gray-headed man who is converted at sixty or seventy finds the remembrance of his youthful sins clinging to him. When he would praise, an old lascivious song revives upon his memory. When he would mount up to heaven, he suddenly remembers some scene in a haunt of vice that he would be glad to forget. But you, saved by divine grace before you thus fall into the jaw of the lion or under the paw of the bear, will certainly have cause for rejoicing all your life.

If I may have heavenly music upon earth let me begin it now, Lord. Put not away the viola and the harp for my fingers when they tremble with age. Let me use them while yet I am young. Now, Lord, if there be a banquet, do not bring me in at the very end of the feast, but let me begin to feast today. If I am to be married to Jesus, let it not be when my hair is gray, but marry me to Jesus now. What better time for joy than today? Now shall my joys swell and grow like a river that rolls on to a mightier breadth and depth as its course is prolonged! I shall rejoice and be glad in You all my days, good Lord, if You will now begin with me in this the morning of my days.

I cannot put my thoughts together this morning as I

could desire, but I still feel an earnest longing to shoot the arrow to its mark. Therefore, one or two stray thoughts before I turn to the prayer itself and these shall be very brief.

My dear young friends, you who are of my own age or younger still, I beseech you ask to be satisfied with God's mercy early, *for you may die early*. It has been our grief this week to stand by the open grave of one who was, alas! too soon, as we thought, snatched away to heaven. You may never number the full ripe years of manhood. We say that our years are threescore and ten, but to you they may not even be a score. Your sun may go down while it is yet noon. God often reaps His corn green; long before the autumn comes He cuts down His sheaves. "Because I will do this, prepare to meet thy God."

Then, on the other hand, if you should live, *in whose service could you spend your days better than in the service of God?* What more happy employment, what more blessed position than to be found, like Samuel, a waiting servant upon God while yet you need a mother's care. *Remember how early temptations beset you.* Would you not wish to secure your early days? And how can you cleanse your ways except by taking heed to them according to God's Word? Do you not know, too, *that the church wants you?* Your young blood shall keep her veins full of vigor and make her sinews strong.

Should not the love of Jesus Christ win you? If He died and shed His blood for men, does He not deserve their best service? Would you desire to give to God an offering of the very end of your days? What would you have thought of the Jew who brought an old bullock—who, after having used an ox in his own fields until it was worn out, should then consecrate it to God? Let the lambs be offered. Let the firstlings of the herd be brought. Let God have the first sheaves of the harvest. Surely He deserves something better than to have the Devil's leavings put upon His holy altar!

"Oh! but," you say, "would He accept me if I came to Him early?" Why, you have more promises than the old man has. It is written that God will be found of them that seek Him, but it is specially written, "They that seek me early shall find me." You have a peculiar promise given to you. If there were any who could be rejected, it could not by any possibility be the young. If there were one whom Jesus Christ could leave, it would not be you, for He gathers the lambs in His bosom. "Suffer the little children to come unto me, and forbid them not, for of such is the kingdom of heaven." May not that cheer you, however young you be? Jesus Christ loves to see young men and women join in His praise. We find that the best of saints in the Old and New Testament were those who came to Jesus young.

Certain it is that the pick and cream of the church in modern times will be found among those who are early converts. Look at those who are church officers and ministers—and the exception only proves the rule. In most cases the leaders in our Israel are those who, as young Hannibal was devoted by his parents to the great cause of his country, were devoted by their parents to the great cause of Zion and to the interests of Jerusalem. If you would be strong for God, eminent in His service, and joyful in His ways, if you would understand the heights and depths of the love of Christ that passes knowledge, if you would give yourselves before your bones are broken and before your spirit has become tinctured through and through with habits of iniquity, then offer this prayer: "O satisfy us early with thy mercy; that we may rejoice and be glad all our days.

A Model for Your Address to God

Every word here is significant. "O"—this teaches us that the prayer is to be earnest. I will suppose that I have led some of you young people here now to breathe this prayer to God. Am I so unhappy as to suppose that none of you will do it? Are there not some who now say, "I will with my whole heart, God the Holy Spirit helping me, now in my pew offer this supplication to heaven." It begins with an "O." Dull prayers will never reach God's throne. What comes from our heart coldly can never get to God's heart. Dull, dead prayers ask God to deny them.

We must pray out of our very souls. The soul of our prayer must be the prayer of our soul. "*O* satisfy us." Young person, the Lord is willing to open the door to those who knock, but you must knock hard. He is fully prepared to give to those who ask, but you must ask earnestly. The kingdom of heaven suffers violence. It is not a gentle grasp that will avail. You must *wrestle* with the angel. Give no sleep to your eyes nor slumber to your eyelids until you have found the Savior.

Remember, if you do but find Him, it will well repay you though you shed drops of blood in the pursuit. If instead of tears you had given your heart's gore, if instead of sighs you were to give the shrieks of a martyr, it would well recompense you if you did but find Jesus; therefore be earnest. If you find Him not, remember you perish, and perish with a great destruction; the wrath of God abides on you, and hell must be your portion. Therefore, as one that pleads for his life so plead for mercy. Throw your whole spirit into it, and let that spirit be heated to a glowing heat. Be not satisfied to stand at the foot of the throne, and say, "Let God save me if He will." No, but put it thus; "Lord, I cannot take a denial. *O* satisfy me; *O* save me." Such a prayer is sure to be accepted.

Again, *make it a generous prayer* when you are at it. "O satisfy *us* early!" I am glad to see among our young sisters in the catechumen class such a spirit of love for one another, so that when one is converted she is sure to look around for another. The scores in that class who have found the Lord are always searching out some stray young woman in the street, or some hopeful ones attending the congregation, whom they try to bring in that Jesus may be glorified. The very first duty of a convert is to labor for the conversion of others. Surely it will not spoil your prayer young man if when you are praying for yourself you will put it in the plural—"O satisfy *us*."

Pray for your brothers and sisters. I am sure we are verily guilty in this thing. Those that sprang from the same loins as ourselves wish to God that they were all saved with the same salvation. You may, some of you, be happy enough to be members of a family in which all are converted. Oh that we could all say the same! May the remembrance of this text provoke you and me to pray for unconverted brothers and sisters more than we have ever done. "O satisfy *us*." If You have brought in the eldest, Lord, stay not until the youngest be converted. If my brother preaches the Word, if my sister rejoices in Your fear, then let other sisters know and taste of Your love. You young people in shops, in warehouses, in factories pray this prayer. Do not exclude even those who have begun to blaspheme, but even in their early youth pray for them—"O satisfy *us* with thy mercy."

See to it, dear friends, in the next place *that your prayer be thoroughly evangelical*. "O satisfy us early *with thy mercy*." The prayer of the publican is the model for us all. No matter how amiable or how excellent we may be, we must all come together and say, "God, be merciful to me a sinner." Do not come with any hereditary godliness. Do not approach the Lord with the fact of your infant sprinkling. Do not come before Him to plead your mother's covenant. Come as a sinner—as a black, foul, filthy sinner—having nothing to rely on or to trust to but the merit of God in Christ Jesus. Let the prayer be just such as a thief might offer or a prostitute might present— "O satisfy us early with thy mercy."

Let the prayer be put up now *at once*. The text says, "O satisfy us *early*." Why not today? Oh that it had been done years ago! But there was time enough you thought. There is time enough, but there is none to spare. Acquaint yourself *now* with God and be at peace. "Today is the accepted time; today is the day of salvation." I would to God we would not pray our prayers meaning to have them heard so late. Let it be: "O satisfy us *early*." The man who truly repents always wants to have pardon on the spot. He feels as if he could not rise from his knees until God has been favorable to him. Mark you, when a man has really come to that point that he must be saved now or else he feels that it will be too late, then has come the solemn juncture when God will say, "Be it unto thee even as thou wilt."

I must leave this poor sermon of mine with the people

of God to pray over it. Sometimes when I long most to plead with men's souls I find the brain distracted although the heart is warm. God knows if I could plead with the young, I would do it even to tears. I do feel it such a solemn thing for our country. Happy shall she be if her sons and daughters give their young days to God! It will be such a blessed thing for London if our young men in business and our young women in families become missionaries for Christ. But what a happy thing it will be for them! What joy shall they know! What transports shall they feel! What a blessing will they be to their households! What happy families they will be! Unconverted fathers shall be made to feel the power of godliness through their daughters. And mothers who despise religion shall not dare to neglect it any longer because they see it exemplified and illustrated in their sons.

We want missionaries everywhere. This great city never can by any possibility become the Lord's except by individual action. We must have all Christians at work. Since we cannot get the old ones to work as we would, since preach as we may, they will settle on their lees, we long for new recruits whose ardor shall rekindle the dying enthusiasm of the seniors. We want to see fresh minds come in all aglow with holy fervor to keep the fire still blazing on the altar. For Jesus Christ's sake I do implore you, you who number but few years, offer this supplication in your pew. Do it now. It is a brother's heart that begs the favor. It is for your own soul's sake that you may be blessed on earth, and that you may have the joys of heaven. There is a prayer-bearing God. The mercy seat is still open. Christ still waits. May the Spirit of God compel you now to come before Him in supplication. Now may He compel you to come in with this as your cry, "O satisfy us early with thy mercy; that we may rejoice and be glad all our days."

NOTES

The Crime of Being Young

Clovis Gillham Chappell (1882–1972) was one of
American Methodism's best-known and most effective
preachers. He pastored churches in Washington, D.C.;
Dallas and Houston, Texas; Memphis, Tennessee; and
Birmingham, Alabama; and his pulpit ministry drew
great crowds. He was especially known for his
biographical sermons that made biblical figures live and
speak to our modern day. He published about thirty
volumes of sermons.

This message was taken from *Chappell's Special Day
Sermons*.

Clovis Gillham Chappell

6

THE CRIME OF BEING YOUNG

He despised him for his youth (1 Samuel 17:42 *Moffatt*).

The Arrival of David

Here is a story so gripping and human that it will live
forever. Israel is being invaded by an old and persistent
enemy, the Philistines. When the armies stand facing
each other, a champion comes forward from the ranks of
the Philistines and proposes to settle the issue by single
combat. Such contests, as you know, were quite common
in classical and medieval times. This champion was all
that could be desired in the way of brute force. He was
nine feet in height. He had a coat of mail that weighed
one hundred and fifty pounds. He had a spear like a
weaver's beam and a voice like the roar of a lion. At his
challenge, the knees of the most heroic in the army of
Israel went weak, and no man dared fight him. Each day
this champion renewed his challenge, becoming all the
while more arrogant and bold and insulting. Each day
the Israelites refused to accept, thus weakening their
morale and becoming more cowed and shamed and
hopeless.

At last after forty days of humiliation, reinforcements
came. How many a tragic day has been saved by the coming of reinforcements! There was a time when the battle
of Waterloo seemed lost to the forces of Wellington. Napoleon was so sure that he had won the day that he went
so far as to dispatch a runner to Paris to tell that the
victory was his. Then, reinforcements came to the Iron
Duke and Napoleon's victory was changed into defeat.
When the armies of the Allies were hard pressed during
the World War, about the sweetest music that they ever
heard was that rather crude song, "The Yanks Are Coming!" It brought new hope to a million hearts.

That should have been the case when David came. His arrival was to mean the dawning of a new day. But nobody believed it. Goliath, the champion, looked upon him with utter contempt. This would not have been so bad had his contempt not been shared by the soldiers on both sides of the line. This contempt found its fullest expression in the biting words of David's own elder brother Eliab. Saul was more friendly, but the best he could do was to look wistfully at the young fellow and shake his head. He was desperately eager for a champion, but he could see no hope here. "Thou art not able," he murmurs sadly, "for thou art but a youth." What was wrong with David? What was his crime? Why did they receive him with such an utter lack of enthusiasm? There seems only one answer: He was guilty of being young.

Now, age and youth have always had a tendency to clash. Here, for instance, is a story that comes out of the book of Ezra. After Jerusalem had been conquered and her people carried away into exile, it was the fondest dream of certain pious and patriotic Jews that they might once again return to Jerusalem to rebuild their ruined city and restore their desecrated temple. After long years of waiting, their dream has been so far realized that a handful of them has returned and restored the walls have and in some measure rebuilt the city. And now they have come to that which was the very climax of their hopes. They are laying the foundation of the temple. When this was done there went up a loud shout of sheer joy. But mingled with this shout of joy were the sobbings of some who seemed utterly brokenhearted. Who were doing the shouting? It was the youth. They were looking ahead. They were thinking what a glorious temple theirs was to be and how sure they were to meet God in it in the days to come. It was the old folks that were sobbing. They were thinking of the temple that they knew when they were young. It was so much bigger and more beautiful than this one that a glimpse of it through the haze of memory made them burst into tears.

This clash of age with youth is quite vigorously alive today. You young people certainly have us worried. We are wondering just what you are going to do next. Not a few of us elders feel that you are about the worst generation the world has yet seen. Then there is little doubt that we are worrying you, not greatly, but enough to be annoying. We are making you wonder just how you are going to get it across to us that we have forgotten the score, lost step, and are at least a half century behind the times. How can you let us know, without hurting us too much, that we are just fossils—kindly fossils maybe; at times harsh and stupid fossils, perhaps; but fossils nonetheless.

Now, while this age-old conflict between age and youth is easy to explain, it is hard to correct. It is so difficult to get springtime and autumn to see each other's viewpoint. You who are young have never been old. Therefore it is hard for you to put yourselves in our places. It is hard for you to realize that soon you, with your burdens and wrinkles and graying hair, will seem prosaic to your juniors as we to you. Then we who are older have such a tremendous tendency to forget that we were ever young. Once we knew everything, even as you. Once, too, we were not absolutely perfect, as surprising as that confession may seem. We forget this and, therefore, fail to put ourselves in your places. Thus our attitude too often becomes one of carping criticism rather than one of sympathy. It was so in the case of David in the long ago. When he came forward eager to help, his elders tried to kill his enthusiasm by finding fault.

The Charges Against David

Look at the charges brought against youthful David. They have a decidedly modern flavor about them.

David is accused of seeking a big job while he is making a mess of the one he has. "Why are you here?" asks his indignant brother. "With whom have you left those few poor sheep?" What Eliab means is that David simply will not settle down to the faithful performance of his duty. "You do not stick to your job," he tells him, "as I did when I was a boy." What a familiar falsehood that is, and how utterly useless! "You are bent on beginning at the top," he continues. "You want to build a spire without taking time to lay a foundation. You are eager to get into a hogshead when, as a matter of fact, you are rattling around in the shell of a mustard seed. You must start at the bottom and work up, as I did."

Now, this is a serious charge. This is the case because the only sure way to get ready for tomorrow is to be faithful in the use of today. The best road into a bigger job is the making the most possible out of one that is small. Some of our youth forget this. But David did not. He may have had just a few sheep, but he kept them faithfully. When one night a bear came after one of his lambs, the bear did not get the lamb, but David got the bear. The story is the same when a lion had undertaken a raid on his flock. Though his task was small, and though it was performed under no human eye, he did it faithfully and well, even at the cost of risking his life.

David is accused of being forward. "I know your forwardness," says this angry elder brother. "I know how confident you are, how certain you are that you know everything. You have absolutely no respect for your elders. You have no reverence for anything nor anybody." That, too, sounds a bit familiar. It is what many of us are thinking of modern youth, and not without reason. It was in some measure true of David. It is possibly yet more true of the youth of today. Certainly you who are young have no disposition to flatter your elders by your too high regard for their opinions. You shock us by your discussions of subjects once taboo. You shock us even more by your frank confession of delinquencies that our generation would never have thought of confessing. Then when we become alarmed, you regard us with about as much seriousness as a young duck disporting itself upon a pond would manifest toward a fussy old hen that was frantic with fear lest her adopted offspring might not be able to swim. Yes, youth is usually a bit forward. But that is not altogether bad. The certainty that you can improve upon your elders is one of the secrets of your strength.

Another charge against David is that of self-will. "I know your self-will," says this indignant brother. "You are bent on having your own way. You are determined to live your own life, to do absolutely as you please." This is a charge that is especially up-to-date. We seem to be in the midst of a veritable revelry of doing as we please. We are at present about the most lawless nation on the earth. Our biggest single business is crime. The majority of those engaged in the crime business are young. The average age of our present-day criminal is only nineteen years. Self-will is certainly, therefore, one of the besetting sins of the youth of today.

But in this our young people are far more sinned against than sinning. The tragic breakdown did not begin with them, but further back. Many of the safeguards that we older folks knew in our youth have become greatly weakened, or have been thrown into the trash. For instance, our generation has witnessed a weakening of the restraints born of religion. "Where there is no vision, the people cast off restraint." Vast numbers of us elders have lost all sense of God, and have, therefore, cast off restraint. This has told upon our home life. Many of our youth are but shattered fragments of broken homes. Others come from homes where there is no serious effort at right training, either by precept or example. Where self-will is the law of life for so many fathers and mothers, it is not surprising that it has put its defiling touch upon some of our youth.

The final charge against David is that he is not serious. He is a mere thrill hunter. He cares for nothing but a good time. For instance, he has come to the front just to see the battle. He cares nothing for the outcome. It matters not to him whether Israel wins or loses, rises to honor or sinks into shame. All he is concerned about is the thrill of seeing the battle. He is forever seeking something that will pack a punch, that will give him a kick. So age has been prone to think of youth through the centuries. There are many today who are ready to bewail the fact that our young people are so dreadfully wanting in seriousness, that they are so thoroughly flippant. It is a serious charge, and one that is far older than the story of this youthful shepherd lad.

The Truth About David

But what is the truth about David, as we learn it, not from his critics, but from his own conduct?

He is tremendously in earnest. True, he is quite young. The roses of springtime bloom upon his cheeks and the light of morning sparkles in his eye. Yet he is not flippant. Saul himself is hardly more deeply concerned for the destinies of Israel than he. And somewhat of this deep seriousness we dare claim for the youth of today. We have all passed, during recent years, through a bit of a fiery furnace. Nor have any of us come out altogether without the smell of fire upon our garments. Youth bears its wounds and scars even as you and I. But whatever faults we may charge against them, flippancy is not one of them. Not for long, I dare say, has there been a generation of youth more genuinely serious than the one with which we are privileged to work. This is in itself greatly hopeful.

Then David has a capacity for a fine moral indignation. When he hears the insulting challenge of this giant of brute force, he expects to see the hand of every soldier of Israel leap to the sword. He expects to see every man on tiptoe of eagerness for battle. But when he realizes that the only response that they dare to make to the swaggering bully is a tame and spineless submission, his expectancy gives way to shame, and his shame to hot anger. "Who is this uncircumcised Philistine," he asks with glowing cheeks and flashing eyes, "that he should defy the armies of the living God?" We like these brave and burning words, all of us. We are glad to see David refuse to worship the god of things as they are. We rejoice that he will not allow bullying wrongs to go unchallenged today just because they went unchallenged yesterday.

Now, this capacity to blaze against wrong has been a characteristic of youth at its best through the centuries. It is one of the most heartening facts of our day. Social injustice, race prejudice, the hell and madness of war are being challenged and fought today as never before. This is preeminently a youth movement. By this I do not mean that all who are engaged in it are young in years. But real youth is not a mere matter of the almanac, it is a matter of the heart. As long as we can rise against wrong in hot indignation, we have youth, whatever the calendar may say. But when we come tamely to submit, that means that we are old, however few our birthdays.

> The lamp of youth will be clean burnt out,
> But we will subsist on the smell of it.
> Whatever we do, we will fold our hands,
> And suck our gums, and think well of it.
> Yes, we shall be perfectly pleased with
> ourselves
> And that is the perfectest hell of it.

Finally, David is possessed of that high virtue that is universally admired. He has courage. It is fine to be in earnest about the things that count. It is fine to be able to burn with a clean indignation against wrong. But even all this is not enough. We must have the grit to do something about it. David might have given vent to his indignation by merely criticizing his elders as they had criticized him. He might have squandered his energies in boasting what he would do in their place or what he was going to do when he was older and better prepared. But he does not wait for some easy tomorrow when the odds against him might not be so great. With a fine madness that stirs our hearts, he offers to do battle then and there. Then and there he takes upon himself the weighty task of doing the impossible. That is the call to the youth of today. To answer it requires courage of the highest order.

How has David come by such courage? It was not born of his consciousness of superior strength. No more was it the result of his belief in the superiority of his equipment. He knows that in these he is no match for Goliath. His courage was born of his faith in God. He believes that the supreme forces are those that are spiritual. "Thou comest to me with a sword and spear and shield, but I am come to thee in the name of the LORD of hosts, the God of the armies of Israel whom thou hast defied." Here is the secret of courage at its highest and best. "I have set the Lord always before me. Because he is at my right hand I shall not be moved." In the courage born of faith, this youth went forth to battle and to victory.

And now the scene shifts from that far-off time to our desperate and difficult days. Colossal wrongs still stalk abroad, and gigantic evils loll about us unafraid. In our need we appeal to you who are young. It is up to you to help bring in a better day. To this end you were born, and for this cause you came into the world. Of course, you may refuse to heed the call. You may take a coward's way and bewail the fact that the times are out of joint and that you were ever born to set them right. But you may also take the way of faith and courage and throw yourselves wholeheartedly into the fight. If you do this, as I believe you will, your very difficulties will become advantages. You will be enabled to sing with joy as you zestfully press the battle:

> Blest is it in this dawn to be alive;
> But to be young, is very heaven.

NOTES

A Young Man and His Perils

George W. Truett (1867–1944) was perhaps the best-known Southern Baptist preacher of his day. He pastored the First Baptist Church of Dallas, Texas, from 1897 until his death and saw it grow both in size and influence. Active in denominational ministry, Truett served as president of the Southern Baptist Convention and for five years was president of the Baptist World Alliance, but he was known primarily as a gifted preacher and evangelist. Nearly a dozen books of his sermons were published.

This sermon was taken from *The Prophet's Mantle,* published in 1948 by Broadman Press.

George W. Truett

7

A YOUNG MAN AND HIS PERILS

And the king said unto Cushi, Is the young man Absalom safe? (2 Samuel 18:32).

EVERY LORD'S DAY, many young men find their way to this place of prayer and worship, and many young women as well. The coming of both these classes touches all our hearts very deeply, and touches the preacher's heart profoundly. I find myself every Lord's day evening—as my eye sweeps this group of young men and women, and every Lord's day morning as well—wondering how things are going with our young men and our young women. I do not have words to tell you, my young friends, how intense is my concern that the best may be your portion. I know something of the battles and the struggles that are incident to a young man's life. My heart overflows with deepest and most prayerful sympathy for our young men. In fancy, I follow you as you go away every Sunday morning and evening from this place, treading the labyrinths of this modern and fast growing city. I follow you and wonder how it is when you get to your rooms, when you are alone, and when you are with others. I wonder how goes the battle of life and if you are living life like it ought to be lived.

I bring you this evening an old question to accentuate the interest felt in young life and to give emphasis to its value while yet life is young. It is from 2 Samuel 18:32:

And the king said unto Cushi, Is the young man Absalom safe?

You need to get this scene before you. Tonight, when you shall have gone home, it will be well for you to read several chapters in the second book of Samuel, that the scene may be entirely before you. Absalom, son of David the King, proved utterly disloyal and treacherous to his father. You will not read in the Bible a more despicable story than that of Absalom lifting up his heel against his own father. You will feel indignation as you contemplate the conduct of this young man, who flung to the winds every motive that should obtain in a son's heart toward his father. It is one of the most wretched stories ever penned for our instruction and warning.

You will observe as you read it that ambition of the wrong kind led Absalom the downward way. There is an ambition of the right kind. The Bible speaks of the right kind of ambition. Paul spoke of a certain ambition he had. It was the right kind. It was inspiring, noble, unselfish. It was in its very essence the desire to be serviceable in the largest way to others. Ambition of that kind is entirely legitimate and praiseworthy, and its fires are to be fed and fanned constantly. But Absalom's ambition was earthward and downward and perditionward. He desired his father's throne. His father was king of Israel. He desired his father's renown, his father's prestige, his father's popularity, his father's power, his father's place. Swept on by that desire, he went to the lowest and most ignoble depths.

Beware of the wrong kind of ambition. Take no short cuts at any time to gain your point. If by telling a lie tonight you could make around a billion dollars, you would be poor beyond speech if you told the lie and got the billion dollars. Take no short cuts. Let no false ambition play tricks on you and dig ditches for you and tie ropes around your necks. Let your ambition be such as may be smiled upon by Him, who is infinite in righteousness and holiness and wisdom.

The evil ambition hurled a great circle of angels out of heaven above us. Selfish ambition plunged even Christ's apostles into serious trouble time and again. The wrong kind of ambition will make mischief even in the holy sanctuary, even in the pulpit. It plays havoc, sows dragon's teeth, kindles fires of untold distress. Beware of the wrong kind of ambition. The stultifying of conscience, the deadening of the finer powers of the moral nature, to gain a point, is the wrong kind of ambition.

Absalom did to the death every fine instinct of a man's heart. You recall how he went about his treacherous work. He stood there in the gate of the city, and, as the men would come to see his father the king with their stories of injustice and oppression and wrong treatment, he would call them and bewail the fact that he was not a judge because his heart was burning, he said, to mete out justice and judgment to every man that had a case. He loved the people. He was very compassionate toward unfortunate people, so he said.

Thus, with words oily and honeyed and treacherous, he stole away the hearts of the men from his own father. And the gruesome picture is given us here that when he would make these speeches, as I have indicated, to the men, he would draw them to him and kiss them. Great spectacle! There are men now who kiss the babies and say lovely things to their mothers, who have exactly the spirit of this young man Absalom.

And then you remember, the revolt came, and the armies were joined in battle. The armies of the king and the armies of the treacherous son met in mortal combat, and the issues were fiery and terrible. The king waited there by the gate for the news of the issue of the battle. And, lo, one comes, Cushi by name, and as he draws near the king, he shouts: "Tidings, my lord, tidings!"

You will notice that David did not ask: "Who has won the victory?" He did not ask: "Which side is in possession of the field?" He did not ask: "Has Joab led the forces to triumph?" He did not ask: "Are my men, my soldiers, my loyal subjects, spared?" All that was forgotten and the father-heart asserted itself. We talk about the mother-heart. There is a father-heart as well. The father-heart asserted itself, and David said to Cushi: "Is the young man Absalom safe?"—that vagabond, that traitor, that son lifting up his heel against his father, seeking to murder his father and destroy everything in the kingdom which his father sought to build up. The father-heart asserted itself, and he cried to Cushi: "Is the young man Absalom safe?" Exultingly Cushi answered: "The enemies of my lord the king, and all that rise against thee to do thee hurt be as that young man is." And then David knew that his son was dead, and there was a pathos in his utterance that can be felt yet. He went up to his chamber over the gate, and over and over and over and over he wailed out his cry: "Oh, my son, Absalom, my son, my son Absalom! Would God I had died for thee, O Absalom, my son, my son!" You can feel it yet. You do not wonder that Longfellow phrased in verse that same idea:

> Is it far from thee
> Thou canst no longer see
> In the chamber over the gate
> That old man desolate:
> Weeping and wailing sore
> For his son who is no more?
> O, Absalom my son!

> Somewhere at every hour
> The watchman on the tower,
> Looks forth to see the fleet
> Approach of the hurrying feet,
> Of messengers that bear
> The tidings of despair.
> O, Absalom, my son!

> That 'tis a common grief
> Brings but slight relief.
> Ours is the bitterest loss,
> Ours is the heaviest cross
> And forever the cry will be:
> "Would God I had died for thee,
> O, Absalom, my son!"

Now what of this question that David asked: "Is the young man Absalom safe?" First of all it was a question a father asked about his son. Oh, what anxieties are burning ever in the hearts of true parents, whether father or mother! What anxieties parents feel for their children! These anxieties are whetted and sharpened and intensified with the passing days. What anxieties parents feel for their children! If only the children could realize this, a thousand chapters of ingratitude would not be

written and tearful searchings of heart would be spared
parents.

A man went across this country, from one side of it
to the other awhile ago. As he was getting off at a little
station in the northeast, the conductor asked him: "Why
do you get off here?" And the man said: "I broke my
mother's heart long years ago. I did not know it then. I
know it now. But I have come back now and want to go
out to the grave where she has slept for years and years.
I want to kiss the ground above her body and beg her,
now cold in death, to forgive me, even yet." Oh, if children knew the griefs they cause their parents. If they
knew how much parents bear in silence. If they knew
how much parents toss when the children sleep because
there was a chapter written by the child that ought
never to have been written! If they only knew! If they
only knew!

When we turn to the Word of God some of its greatest
utterances are to children, summoning them to remember their right relation to their parents. One of the great
pronouncements from Jehovah for our consideration is:
"Honor thy father and thy mother, that thy days may be
long upon the land which the LORD thy God giveth thee."
To that great command of proper honor upon the part of
children toward their parents is attached, as you see, a
great promise—a promise of blessing, a promise of grace,
and a promise of goodness and mercy.

And then again God pronounces one of His direst
curses against children who mistreat their parents. In
one place He tells us that if the child shall look with scorn
toward his father and shall despise the counsel of his
mother, the day comes on apace when the eagle will pluck
out such child's eyes, so horrible is such child's sin. The
note ought to be sounded from border to border in this
country, that homes are to be controlled by the parents
and not by the children. The right kind of respect upon
the part of the child toward the parent goes a long way
toward prophesying beautiful days out yonder. But dis-
loyalty, disrespect, and disobedience upon the part of the
child toward the parent will cause agony and regret and

pain and tears. Remorse, which burns like fire on the altar of memory, will take its toll.

From the cradle to the grave parents are interested in their children, and these children are always their children. No matter to what height they rise nor to what depth they fall, still the parental heart overflows with anxiety toward such children. I have seen an example of it today that touched my heart to its deepest depth. The child had not been sufficiently considerate, and coming from another city was a parent who said: "I do not know that my visit will be properly received. But I come to be near and to say, if I can, some word even in this dark hour to help a disobedient child. I want to be near to do everything I can." The interest of the parent lasts on and on, even though the child be estranged from home.

In my mail yesterday came letters, as almost daily letters come, from parents who are anxious about their children. One mother was asking that I go to see her son. She said: "He has not written me now for long, long months. I do not know why. My pillow is wet with tears each night because I cannot hear from him. You will please find out why he does not write. He is working at such and such a place. You will gently tell him that I have written you, that I can wait no longer. I must hear from him." And then, another wrote: "My child, the last I heard, was in your city, and he was in trouble. I do not know where he is now. All I can do is to call to God in his behalf. I am going to pray that you may find him and speak the right word to him." Oh, it is like that constantly, the anxiety of a parent thus expressing itself for an absent child.

This question of our text was asked by a father concerning his son—his son away from home, his son in dire rebellion against his father. Oh, to what lengths parental love will go! The worst enemy David had on earth that same day was Absalom, his son. Absalom had every foul thing in his heart toward David. He meant to rob David of his crown. He meant David's destruction. He meant David's humiliation and shame and death. Yet though he meant all of that, and the father knew that his boy meant all that, he asked this plaintive question: "Is my boy safe?" That villain, that traitor, that deceiver, that son incarnate in his fiendishness, is he safe? Oh to what lengths parental concern will go for a child!

But David asked his question too late. Absalom was not safe. Three darts aimed by Joab had pierced through his body. Absalom, handsome Absalom, lay dead, and his name was to be shrouded with disgrace throughout eternity. You can ask that question too late. The time to ask it is before the shadow falls. The time to ask it is not to be overlooked and not to be forgotten. David asked it too late!

When is a young man or a young woman not safe? Such a person is not safe if in wrong relation to his or her parents. Any son in wrong relation to his parents is not safe. He is on dangerous ground, ground that is nothing more than quicksand. He is challenging the wrath of Almighty God. Any man or woman in wrong relation to his or her parents, no matter how old, nor how old-fashioned, nor how inconsiderate and unreasonable such parents may be, is in danger of being swallowed up by the quicksands of dishonor and shame and condemnation from Him who said: "Honor thy father and thy mother." If I speak tonight to one in this place who is in any way in wrong relation toward the old folk at home, oh, I pray you, hasten to readjust that wrong relation.

When is the young man not safe? He is not safe when going with the wrong kind of company. To an awful degree our companionships make us or mar us in our earthly lives. The Bible tells us so. The Word says: "He that walketh with wise men shall be wise" and it adds, "but the companion of fools shall be destroyed." Frequently I have seen young men, in these years I have been in this goodly city of Dallas, come here, their faces fresh with the freshness of the ripening peach and their eyes clear with the purity of the blue sky above us. Yet, through influences set up by wrong companionships, they have sunk into the morass of evil ways. Their fate and their depths are now too terrible almost for human speech. "Evil communications corrupt good manners." A man's life is very largely made or very largely marred by his companionships. If he chooses evil companions, he will imbibe their spirit. If he goes with the right kind, even so will he be blessed by their spirit. A young man is not safe and a young woman is not safe who is in the wrong kind of company. A young woman asked me recently: "Should I keep company with a young man who scorns religion?" I said: "I strongly advise against that. You will jeopardize your own peace of mind and heart. You will imperil your own faith, your own religion, your own soul if you should become yoked with a scorner of religion. You can earnestly pray for that young man that he may be converted, but do not choose him as your life companion so long as he remains a scoffer of Christ and His blessed religion. Paul gave wise advice when he wrote the Christians of Corinth saying: 'Be not unequally yoked with unbelievers.'"

When is the young man not safe? The young man is not safe when he has the wrong kind of habits in his life. Read the story of this young man, Absalom. You will see how he, handsome and daring and reckless and charming, was weighted down with the wrong kind of habits. For one thing, his extravagance was flagrant and glaring, even appalling. The record here tells us that he hired chariots and horses, and had fifty young men to run before him to do obeisance to him, to flatter him, to pamper him, to coddle him, to boost him. Whenever a young man has extravagant habits, he is digging a pit for himself out yonder somewhere into which he will fall.

It may seem strange counsel to you, yet I would urge every young man here, whatever the salary, if it be only a dollar a day, that he save some of that against "the rainy day." The word of discretion, prudence, and forethought suggests that every man shall live within his means. Men should remember that. If you have the extravagant habit and let it dominate your life, the day is not far distant when that habit will bring disaster to your life.

Any young man's life is imperiled who yields to a wrong habit. Maybe the habit is one of idleness. That habit is menacing and undoing. The idle man is a dangerous one.

He is a menace to his community, to his state, and to the social order. If I were out of a job, I would break stones on the streets at ten cents an hour before I would be idle. Men who go here and there, idly beating their way, able to work, ought to be condemned by every right thinking man in the community. The idler is a menace to society. The idler is a parasite. The idler is a fraud. The idler is a cheat. The idler is a distinct scourge to any community. If a young man is idle then there is mischief brewing for him and the people in his circle. The rich man ought not to be willing to live the idle life, nor should the idle anybody, because the idler furnishes fruitful occasion for Satan to work exceeding havoc in such person's life. And, young men, you are not to despise the humble task, the modest job. Perform well the duty that lies at hand and before long other doors of opportunity will swing open before you. Performance is the path that leads to promotion. Flee from idleness as from a plague. "Satan finds some mischief still for idle hands to do."

The young man is not safe if he has the habit that is licentious. Ah me, what chapters could be unfolded concerning the down-dragging of young men's lives because the licentious habit in secret was taken up, and it led on to humiliation and fearful disaster. The young man, if he has the licentious habit, is in great peril. The young man is to be pure even as the young woman is to be pure. The so-called double standard is a snare and a delusion. It has wrought untold havoc in the world. The young man is to be clean and untainted and unbesmirched. The young man's life is to be such that he can look his mother, or his sister, or his future wife in the face and be conscious within his own heart that his life is unbefouled by licentious habits. The young man is not safe who allows licentiousness to eat into his life like some foul cancer.

Now I would sum it all up by saying that the young man is not safe if he is not openly and positively God's friend. "Hold Thou me up, and I shall be safe," says God's Word. Nor is there safety anywhere else. No man is able in his own strength to withstand the currents that beat against him. No man is able, in his own strength, to withstand the down-dragging quicksands over which his feet must go. No man is able to cope with Satan and his insidious and seductive wiles in his own strength. No man is able to walk victorious down life's way in his own strength without divine help, no matter how well fortified he may be—no matter how splendid his rearing, no matter how superbly he may have fixed in his life right habits. No young man or young woman is safe if such person is not pronouncedly and honestly on God's side.

Oh, is your life safe? God, who made you, asks that question insistently. Christ, who died for you, asks that question. He who loves you and preserves you and bestows His benefits upon you asks that question: "Is your life safe?" It is not safe if you are in wrong relation toward Him who made you, toward Him who redeemed you, toward Him who preserves you, toward Him who waits and pleads to get your consent that He may be your Savior and Guide and Master and Keeper. Your life cannot be safe unless you are rightly related to Him. Is your soul safe? Is your security for the heavenly life and land already fixed? Are you the friend of Jesus, who is the Savior of sinners? Are you His disciple? Are you His follower? Are you His servant? Do you trust Him and say to Him: "Lead Thou me as Thou wilt?" Are you for Christ? Then your case is safe and the main thing has been settled, a position has been taken, and your destiny has been already determined, if you are for Christ.

Do you say: "I am not for Him, but I wish to be?" Hasten, I pray you, to decide for Christ. Hasten to make your surrender to Christ. Hasten to be on Christ's side. Hasten to cut all the cables that hold you, to burn all the barriers that separate you from Christ. Hasten to come out of the valley of waiting and indecision and inaction. Hasten to surrender to Christ. Decide now for Christ! He is the way, and the truth, and the life. In Him is safety and salvation and victory for this world and for the world to come. Register your decision now!

NOTES

The Clash of Age and Youth

Arthur John Gossip (1873–1954) pastored churches in England and Scotland before becoming Professor of Practical Theology at Trinity College, Glasgow. He gave the Warrack Lectures on Preaching in 1925, published under the title *In Christ's Stead,* and he published several books of sermons. He was not a dramatic preacher, but the intensity of his delivery and the depth of his message and character attracted and held the listeners. Perhaps his most famous sermon is "But When Life Tumbles In, What Then?" which he preached the Sunday after his wife suddenly died after what was supposed to be minor surgery.

This message was taken from his book *The Hero in Thy Soul,* published in 1930 by Charles Scribner's Sons, New York.

Arthur John Gossip

8

THE CLASH OF AGE AND YOUTH

And all the people shouted with a great shout, when they praised the LORD, because the foundation of the house of the LORD was laid. But many of the priests and Levites and chief of the fathers, who were ancient men, that had seen the first house, when the foundation of this house was laid before their eyes, wept with a loud voice; and many shouted aloud for joy: So that the people could not discern the noise of the shout of joy from the noise of the weeping of the people (Ezra 3:11–13).

THE BIBLE WILL NEVER grow out of date for many reasons. One is that every possible mood of the human spirit is photographed in it with such vivid lifelikeness that we catch our breath and stand still. We stare in astonishment at what we ourselves have often felt and seen, but which we had assumed was something peculiar to ourselves, or at least individual to our day—a special characteristic that would always mark it out from other times. Yet here it is, all set down with a startling exactness in the experience of men and women dead thousands of years.

So true is it that we are all much more like each other than we know. Our boasted originalities are only yet one other echo of what has been blowing around the world, common as dust, almost since time began. There were doles in Greece, and wartime prohibition in China, and leagues of nations here and there, centuries before our Lord was born. Disheartening though it may seem, our problems are perennial problems. And what our own hearts in their secret places are today, that, very largely, human hearts have always been.

Here, for example, in this dim corner of the Scriptures, ill lit and but little frequented, suddenly we come upon how telling a picture of that unbridgeable chasm that

105

yawns between one generation and the last—of that noisy clashing between age and youth—the din of which so fills our ears in our own day. We see age with its memories, its wistfulnesses, its regrets; youth with its valiant dissatisfactions, its hot enthusiasms, its confident hopes. The one stands with a shading hand up to its brow, gazing back lingeringly over dear familiar scenes from which it parts reluctantly; the other all impatience to be up and gone, looking out eagerly toward the new day and "with morning in its eyes." So it was then; so it is still; so perhaps it must always be on to the end.

Here, then, is a very real and practical and always pressing problem that needs chivalrous hearts and delicate fingers to handle it, if an unwisely hectoring and censorious experience, fretted by youth's crude and too confident immaturities, is not to nag and scold and sour. If an impatient youth, claiming its independence, is not angrily to fling away into an impudent intolerance, one must not nag and scold and sour. If the happy relationships God planned for both are not to be dimmed and clouded over by bickering, misunderstanding and sheer pettiness, and an unhappy lack of sympathy and seemly self-restraint, one must not nag and scold and sour. "I would," grumbles the testy old shepherd in *The Winter's Tale*, "that there was no age between ten and three-and-twenty, or that youth would sleep out the rest." Certainly that would make a quieter world, but obviously there is no hope in that idea. We must light upon some other better way.

That was a great day in Jerusalem when they laid the foundations of a new temple. For, of all the horrors of the invasion and overthrow, nothing had burned itself so searingly into the people's hearts as the sight of God's house desecrated, fallen, a mere huddled heap of tumbled stones. All through the exile that had haunted them. And now their hands were at last wiping off that insult spat into God's face. The site was cleared of its charred ruins. Here at length was a beginning actually made. A very little longer and the walls would be there, rising before their eyes. It was a dream so old, so dear, for long enough so hopelessly impossible. And it was coming true, was really coming true! At thought of that their hearts spilled over, would not be contained, burst into praise and thanksgiving and a great shout of joy. But amid all that riot of happiness, the older people, who were very happy too, felt something salt and choking suddenly rise up in their throats. They were back for the moment among things that they could never see again: in the old temple of their youth, living again the great and unforgettable days, when they had met God face-to-face there in that stately house of His, back among all that they had known and loved—and lost. This new temple could never mean to them what that other had been.

And indeed how very shabby it was, now they looked at it, and how mean and pitiful its whole design, judged by the standards that they knew. And what else could it be? For what resources had they in their fallen state? Cyrus had promised something; but they could not expect too much from him. So they complained and criticized. And indeed the measurements were trivial, the whole scheme cramped and stunted. It was so brave a dream that they had dreamed. Was it all to end in this poor makeshift of a thing? And with that, in their sudden emotional Oriental way, they burst into a passion of weeping. Until what is that the wind is carrying to us? Is it rejoicing or a sob? Is it a shout of triumph or a wail of hurt things crying out in pain? It is the clash of youth and age, and in one way or another it is heard in every generation.

Still folk are young, still folk are old, and still we all stand at a new beginning. For the world keeps hurrying on. And always some are gazing out ahead with faith and hope and an immense enthusiasm. And always some keep looking back at what they think was better: at the big times, gone now, and, as they feel, leaving only a dull appendix in small print, a sorry anticlimax of a chapter, a mere huddle of stupid nothings like those last lean pages when a man's work is over and he dodders to and fro until the end comes. For surely, they think, God Himself has half retired these meaningless days. Surely men have very noticeably shrunk in stature, have become a pettier breed, have ceased to throw up mighty figures as they always used to do. Surely nothing ever happens nowadays to fire men's blood in the old, wildly glorious way.

Perhaps that cleavage into two was never more apparent than today, and probably not often has there been more obvious reasons for it. Do you remember how, on the Somme, after the little towns and villages had been blown into nothingness until not one stone remained, they set up notice boards that ran: "This was Bazentin le petit"; "'This was Bazentin le grand," and the like? And remember how the whole district had to be rebuilt from the beginning? For ten years now we have been toilsomely building up again a world blown into atoms. We are tired, and hot, and perhaps just a little cross with one another for getting in each other's way. And what do we think of it, this brand-new world that we have fashioned?

Loyally the older people try to keep in step, and to adjust themselves to the new circumstances and environment. They want to like it, yet they are not sure that they do like it. They catch themselves looking back across their shoulders wistfully enough to the old times, as to the place where their heart really dwells. And that is natural enough. They are homesick. For did not Emerson tell us truly that, had any one been born ten years later or earlier than he was, he would have been an altogether different person, because set down in a quite other world, amid quite other thoughts and hopes and ways? And their world with its ways, their ways, is vanishing. Like an emigrant watching his native land fade out forever, with his eyes full of tears and his heart grown unutterably lonely, so they, too, feel lost.

And "when he had served his day and generation," so we read, "he fell asleep." That is the most that nearly anyone can do. And a generation quickly passes, and a day's sun soon sets. There is the time of preparation, and then some five-and-twenty years of work or more, and thereafter most of us begin to lag behind, to get in the way increasingly. More and more we impede the others.

More and more they push us aside, a little roughly and impatiently at last. Oh, get out of the road! they cry. And with a start we recognize, if we are wise, that we have grown old-fashioned, slow, and out of date, and perhaps even a little stupid. And if, as is more likely, we are not too wise, we flare up angrily into a chronic snarl of irritation at being jostled and bustled and elbowed so unceremoniously out of our sober pace.

Stevenson tells us how acutely every Scotsman feels the moment he has crossed the border that he is not in his own land. The church is different, the laws are different, the ways and customs are quite curiously different, the houses are different, the people in their whole make-up are different. It may be only a few miles that he has traveled, and yet he is in another world. And we soon leave our day behind and find ourselves outlanders in another, and not seldom homesick in our minds.

And some ask petulantly why this has to be? Why can't we settle down where we were, well content? Why all this breathless rushing—after what? A distinguished Anglican divine, preaching before the British Association, is reported to have urged that we might well call a halt in this mad running, might well mop our brows and ease this agonizing stitch in our sides. He has urged that we might pass an ordinance to cease from further inquiry into material laws and forces until we have gotten our breath again, and have managed to adjust ourselves to all that we already know. That was a rather futile little bleat. It is obviously hopeless. For the world persists in spinning around and around, and won't stop because you feel giddy. It was a sheer impertinence for Joshua to bid the sun stand still until he had taken care of his affairs. And it won't listen to us if we try that desperate policy. It goes hurrying on and quickly rises upon a new day.

And why not? people used to ask. For we had a delightful idea that an automatic and mechanically perfect evolution had contrived that we were on a kind of moving stairway that kept rising up and up and still up, always leaving what was poorer, always reaching something better and still better. It was a very comfortable axiom that kept our minds quite easy. But it has been a little roughly handled by the facts of life and looks a good deal tashed and worn and frayed these days. Is it common sense to argue that because a thing comes later, it must of necessity be worthier? Can one really hold that everything that happens in this odd mix-up of a world is God's Spirit breaking in? Isn't it nearer truth to think that a dark star rolls around at intervals between us and the bright one, and obscures its light for us? Was it a nobler England in which people found themselves when Charles II and his ugly orgies of unblushing lust swept away Puritanism with its cleanness and its self-control? "Heartily know, when half-gods go, the Gods arrive," trolls Emerson, with characteristic confidence.

But is that always true? Never a doubt of it, they held poor and crude conceptions of Jehovah in those early days in Israel. But was it better when all that was blotted out, and Baal and Moloch and their horrors took its place? Life is too difficult by far to be summed up with adequacy in the smug headline of a copybook. And are things really better nowadays than they were wont to be in the old world we knew? Some question it, and they are not without their evidence. Look back—regretfully—to the old views of the Bible, let us say. Well, they have vanished, for we must follow truth wherever it may lead. Yet they did seem to give to some a certain assurance, a certain feeling of security, of something solid underneath one's feet where now to many there looks only emptiness. And the old habits? They have passed. And for their part they miss them and feel farther off from God without them. And the old modes of stating truth, which often had a reverence about them that seems lost?

Francis Thompson admits that he found the shoulder of Christ too high for him to lean against. But the new generation does not appear to feel that. Rather, it links arms with Christ in the friendliest way; it talks and thinks of the great Comrade. But the old seemly awe that often filled the minds of those who lived with Christ seems gone. And a fine Indian writer, amazedly gazing at us so jaunty and unabashed, maintains passionately that that is what is wrong with modern Western Christianity. He declares with a white heat that the works even of Dr. Glover, of all men—books that have proved a crowded road for many of us back to God, and upon which we have met Him face-to-face—are to him simply irreligious. Here is a man, he cries—a typical representative of the religion of his day—and, face-to-face with Jesus Christ, he talks about His charm and such-like little vivid surface trifles. Quite evidently he is interested, attracted, fascinated, if you will; but he is not upon his knees, is not down on his face before Him. And that is where we ought to be in Jesus' presence! Dr. Glover apart—for to him I too owe hugely—that charge is true of most of us. We are not down upon our knees; we are not lying on our faces. We are not in the mood that wades into the real deeps of Christianity.

I know that every age must link itself to Christ by what it can. I know that in subapostolic times they look to us now as if largely they had missed the whole point and splendor of the faith. They could, they did, work for it, live for it, die for it. Yet they did not seem to understand it very deeply. And so it may be now. A minister wrote to tell me of an epoch-making crisis in his life that has lifted him into a new realm of Christian experience in which the biggest of the promises are his daily facts, and what we take as startling metaphors prove to him to be literally true. And yet he reported that, haunted by a passage in a book that had revealed to him that there is infinitely more for him in Christ than he had taken from Him, he brooded over it for a long time. Yet he made no progress until, going to his knees, he cried: "O Christ of Galilee! O Christ of Gethsemane! O Christ of Calvary, I give all of myself to Thee; give Thou all of Thyself to me"—a fearsome, glorious, heroic prayer. And it was answered with a staggering fullness. Ah! but we are not praying it.

We are prepared and eager to walk with Christ through the sunny days in Galilee, but are we facing with Him the dark mysteries of life? Aye, more, are we remembering that He Himself has said, with a solemn conviction, that unless we are taking our cross upon our shoulders and are following Him some way into the darkness upon Calvary—into His passion of self-sacrifice, into living our life in His way and for His ends—we are not His disciples and cannot be?

Are things really so much better than they were in the old days? Many among us are by no means sure. Well, anyhow, they are gone and won't come again, not in that form ever again. When you sail away to other lands you don't expect to find the peoples in those countries closely approximating to our ways at home. They have their own customs. No more can you, with reason, hope that a new age will look at things as did the one before it. All missionaries tell us that Eastern Christians can never reproduce our Western Christianity. They too must think out the Lord for themselves—"their Lord," as Paul says in his catholic-hearted way, "no less than ours." They must come to Him on their own feet and must look at Him through their own eyes. And each new generation must be given that same liberty. There is indeed no need of giving. It itself claims and takes that as a primary right.

> The old order changeth, yielding place to new,
>   And God fulfils Himself in many ways,
> Lest one good custom should corrupt the world.
>   Comfort thyself.

The lines are threadbare with much handling and yet—even yet—their lesson is not learned.

It is still difficult for older folk to credit that; to act on the assumption it is true; to find, as Tennyson says boldly, comfort in it. Yet we must keep the windows of our mind wide open and must see that our soul is hospitable to new truth. We must not be churlish hosts but, giving the new guests a hearty welcome, must resolutely refuse to shut ourselves into the past. Mr. Birrell, that fine discriminating bookman, at long last grew tired and discouraged. The new books did not meet his taste, seemed trivial and unappetizing. And he slammed the door and locked himself into the company of the great writers of the past, acting out Lamb's doctrine that when he heard a new book praised he read an old one. But after years of that he changed his mind and opened his door to the new claimants knocking at it. He found that he added another province to his wide-flung empire, that he has all the old delightful comrades undiminished in their glory and these new minds too. So it should be with us. The Holy Spirit did not reach the end of what He had to tell us twenty years ago.

Robertson Nicoll, who loathed fresh air, "often declared," says his biographer, "that if he could have his way he would close all windows forever; indeed, he would construct windows in the manner of the intelligent ancients, so that by no possibility could they be opened. He would aver that he meant to ask the railway companies to seal up the windows of some of their compartments, and label such 'Foul Air.' If they did so, he said, they would be astonished at the rush for carriages thus labelled." Well, there are minds like that, that hate fresh air; that love a stuffy, overbreathed atmosphere; that are terrified of draughts even when it is the winds of God that are blowing through the earth. But they cannot be healthy.

Man is as old as his arteries, it is said. He is not. He is as old as his soul. And some souls age so prematurely. By middle life they are gray-haired and dull and drowsy, and at the extreme limit of all that they will ever be. But others remain young in sheer defiance of the years. Always they are eager, expectant, on tiptoe. Every glare of red in the sky is a fire, and they are off to find it—and they do. And this is not only an itch for novelty. It is because quite simply they assume that God is alive and that wonderful news from Him is likely to break through at any moment. And we who are growing older must take pains to learn that art of keeping the mind young, of learning from our juniors.

I don't think these weeping folk helped very much. The mood was natural enough, perhaps, but certainly not overmanly and little likely to do anything except dishearten those around them. And a mind that is perpetually looking back and talking scornfully of all things present as a sad decadence—that is gloomy and pessimistic, that knows the reins have broken in God's hands and that all things are hurtling hideously down to ruin, that keeps clutching the seat nervously, ready to jump when the disaster it is always foreseeing comes—well, it's a rather miserable role to fill, and surely not a little blasphemous. "You that are old," said Falstaff, when himself gray-haired, already too full blown and with petals ready to fall, "you that are old consider not the capacities of us that are young." And there was much more than knavery in Falstaff. That surely is the fitting spirit! "Look not mournfully into the past, for it comes not back again; improve the present while it is thine; go forth to meet the shadowy future without fear and with a brave heart."

But what about you who are young? Ah, well, you can be trying and exasperating too. That airy assumption of yours that all who went before you were incompetent bunglers—that you are the people, and wisdom will die with you, or at least that suddenly the slow, dour thing has blossomed into full flower in your day—is less than just by far to that innumerable company of valiant souls who, with hard breathing, toil and pain and sheer daredevil heroism, won for you with their bare hands nearly all you have inherited. Look again at your possessions, at the simplest of them. And, like David, with that water from the well at Bethlehem which valiant men had risked their lives to bring, you too will feel, in an awed and even ashamed way, that these are vastly too valuable and have cost far too much, to make it seemly you should use them as if they were common nothings. It will make you want rather to pour them out before God, who alone is worthy to receive them—these things how wonderful when you look at them closer. For has it not taken human blood and brains and lives to win each one of them? Don't forget that.

And yet what does the world not owe to youth—to its unnerving audacities, its hot revolts, its open breaks with the engrained and customary, its discontented flouting of the world as it is, its dogmatic certainty that it ought to be—aye and can be—far, far better? Why, that's what keeps the earth alive, the salt that saves it from corrupting into rottenness. When the Master looked about Him for a symbol of the type of heart that He finds hopeful, and with which He feels at home, He took a little child. And youth too stands not far from Him—youth with its big beliefs, its steady and straight-looking eyes, its sunny faith that has no doubts. It's that that keeps this old world of ours young. Don't be disheartened by old fogies chattering doleful criticisms. You be up and at what God has given you to see and do. And may He in His mercy bless you all your valiant days.

The temple you are raising does seem small, yet, after all, it is a temple where there were only ruins. Frankly, there are times when to us older people you younger folk look just irreligious. Then again we know you are not irreligious and that it is simply that your religion is of another type from ours, which is a very different matter and much less momentous. Judged from our angle it does sometimes seem that you are obsessed by the oddest passion of herding into conferences, of telling each other in minute detail just what ought to be done. When that is over, you seem to conclude your part is finished and so settle down, and nothing follows! Nor do you seem to mind. With all your conferences, not often—never indeed for many years—has it been anything like so difficult to find ministers and missionaries, men willing to give their lives. There is by far more talk; there is by far less sacrifice. "Yes, yes," said Chalmers almost irritably, when they praised him for a marvelous oratorical triumph, "but nothing followed, nothing came of it." And without that, to him the thing was useless and an utter failure. But conferences seem to loom before your minds as an end in themselves. "He who would do good to another," said Blake, "must do it in minute particulars. General good is the plea of the scoundrel, the hypocrite, and the flatterer." Like every other, your generation must do good in minute particulars, by individuals, not waiting for the others, but one by one rising and putting themselves into Christ's hands.

Yet, on the other side, you have acuter consciences by far concerning certain social sores. You simply can't understand how we could tolerate them and look at us in a way that we find most uncomfortable. You look at us much as we ourselves were wont to glance scornfully at the pious people who, prior to our day, served God with what they believed to be a convinced and honest earnestness, while yet thrusting little shivering frightened souls of six and eight down for long, dreadful hours into the darkness of the mines. You look on us just as others down the centuries will look back at you, too. For as yet it is a very crude and elementary Christianity we have worked out, which our successors, please God, will leave far behind. Meantime, when you look at us so hotly, we can only say that, though we cannot well explain it now that our eyes have been directed to them, the fact is we did not see these wrongs that so infuriate you—somehow, we never noticed them. "You see," we stammer, "they were always there. Our eyes ran across them." "Well, we do see them," you say grimly, "and we can't stand them—and we won't."

And that is well. Only you seem to be touched by what Raleigh calls the "idiotic simplicity of the revolutionary idea." You seem to imagine that something external, economic, and political can change this tangled world for us into all that it ought to be, while you and I remain just what we were. It won't, says Christ. It is new men that are needed—another you, another I, another all of us—grown into new and Christlike creatures, with His new ways and thoughts and dreams. And you can be quite certain Christ is right. Still you do see that what, because it looked uncomfortably difficult to live, we pushed aside as obvious metaphors, not to be taken literally, are not metaphors but laws that we have got to learn to work out somehow. You are zealous to do something. Your hands itch to begin to build and to change these ruins into a Temple of God. You have indeed set happily to work, and everywhere there is the tinkling of the trowels on the stones, the sound of busy saw and hammer. Well, God bless you and give you good speed!

And what I would say to each of you is that you must be true to the light of your own generation. There is an old prophet who asks indignantly how people can bear to live in their own ceilinged houses while God's house lies in a blackened heap! And in this day of awakened social conscience, of endeavor to be helpful to each other, are you, for your part, going to hold aloof and take no part in the characteristic enterprise of your own age? Are you going to spend your life dully and commonplacely upon your own ends, just as if these new visions had not risen on men's minds, to be so out of date as to think living for oneself is life? Listen to your own contemporaries; look around you for yourself! Is it not plain that God's will is not being done, that God's earth lies in ruins, that God's great plans are largely still to carry through? And are you to have no share in it all?

There was once a day of crisis in Jerusalem. For Uzziah, the father of his people and the great statesman on whose wisdom they had leaned, was dead. It was

> As when a kingly cedar green with boughs
> Goes down with great shout upon the hills,
> And leaves a lonesome place against the sky.

And everyone felt lost. That day a youngish man, bewildered like the rest, went to the Temple to beg God to raise up someone on whom they could lean. And why not you? said God, in sudden and most unexpected answer. And the man gazed astounded, hardly crediting his own heart. Yet, finding it was said in earnest, he rose up to his feet, dazed and stunned but obedient, "Here am I, send me." And today God is saying, Why not you? And you? And you? Christ needs you. Christ appeals to you. Christ follows you, entreating for your help. God made you for the work of your own generation. Don't throw away your chance! Arise and build, and help to make a better world!

And yet you must not mind me saying that the temple that your generation is raising does look somehow small and mean and even poky. No doubt Carlyle declared that "it is better to build a dog hutch than to dream of building a palace." Not surely, if what you are building is for God. And your designs seem less than adequate by far. It does look as if there were something lopsided, something missing, something wrong. What is it that you have left out? The Court of the Gentiles? Ah! you have made that a spacious place. And it was never busier, with all this bustle of social amelioration and reform, this buzzing and this clamor. The Court of the Women? You are taking down the barrier, I see, that used to keep them shut up by themselves and are giving them full access to God's service in the world. The Court of the Men? Yes, here it is. Yet there is something missing. Why, where is the Veil? And where is the Holiest of All? And where is a place in your religion for hush and quiet and God's presence—for devotion and stillness and prayer? Have you made no provisions for these in your plans? Is your design that of a fussy little chapel, a rather grimy brick affair plastered with notices of endless breathless agencies, a homely, busy little place with swing-doors always swinging, with the click of billiard balls in its back settlements, and a smell of stale tea meeting everywhere? Or is it a cathedral, with its stillness and its space, its quiet and its sense of the infinities? There is something lacking at this end! Where is the Holy Place?

When a squire was to be knighted, he spent the whole preceding night in some cathedral face-to-face, alone, with God. And it was from that holy Presence he rode out to his adventures and his high endeavors. Now our ideal, our hope, our source of power, is not that, but organization. We rely on voices, hoarse from much speaking, and on pushfulness, and on untiring energy. We are always, on principle, so hot, so rushed, so perspiring, so set upon efficiency as we misunderstand that term, that we are letting the real central things die out. Your temple does look small! Something is missing at this inner end of it, something that used to be here. Where is the Veil? Where is the Holy Place? None! None! Believe me, you will make little of a religion, however eager and humanitarian it be, that leaves out God.

NOTES

The Perils of the Middle-Aged

George H. Morrison (1866–1928) assisted the great Alexander Whyte in Edinburgh, pastored two churches, and then became pastor in 1902 of the distinguished Wellington Church on University Avenue in Glasgow, Scotland. His preaching drew great crowds; in fact, people had to line up an hour before the services to be sure to get seats in the large auditorium. Morrison was a master of imagination in preaching, yet his messages are solidly biblical.

From his many published volumes of sermons, I have chosen this message, found in *The Wings of the Morning,* published by Hodder and Stoughton, London.

George H. Morrison

9

THE PERILS OF THE MIDDLE-AGED

The destruction that wasteth at noonday (Psalm 91:6).

IN EVERY LITERATURE the life of man is pictured under the symbol of a day. There is something in the rise and setting of the sun that answers so closely to life's start and close that the correspondence has been universally perceived. We speak of the morn of infancy or childhood; we describe old age as the evening of our day; declining years are the afternoon of life; and final efforts the lingering gleams at sunset. It is in such language, drawn from the sphere of day, that we imaginatively describe the facts of life. This being so, you will at once perceive the meaning we may attach to noonday. The noonday of life is the time of middle age, when the morning freshness of youth has passed away. And so "the destruction that wasteth at noonday," whatever be its literal significance, may without any violence be referred to the peculiar temptations of that period. That, then, is the theme which I would speak upon—the perils that beset the middle-aged. I shall not speak directly to the young, nor shall I offer counsel to the old. But I shall address myself more immediately to those who are in the noontide of their days—in the long stretch that we call middle life.

I do so with all the greater readiness because this is a period so often overlooked. For a hundred special sermons to young men, you will scarce find one that appeals to middle age. No doubt there is something to be said for that, for youth is the time of impression and resolve. The preacher feels that if he can influence youth, the trend of the later period is determined. But along with this wise reason goes another, which is as unwise as it is false and which is specially cogent with young ministers. It is the thought that after the storms of youth, middle age is as a

121

quiet haven. It is the thought that youth is very perilous, and middle age comparatively safe. It is the thought that as a man enters manhood he is encompassed by quicksands and hidden rocks and shoals uncharted, but that in middle age all these are past, and the barque has entered quiet and restful waters. I think that nothing could be more untrue than that. I think no outlook could be more pernicious. I am convinced that of all moral perils none are more deadly than the perils of the noonday. And could we but read the story of this city and of the lives in it that in the sight of God have failed, I believe we should find that the sins of middle age have been more disastrous than the sins of youth. On that, then, let me speak a little—on the temptations peculiar to this period. And so may God, who has spared us through our youth, safeguard us from "the destruction that wasteth at noonday."

Now one of the great features of middle age is this— and, of course, I can only speak in general terms—that by that time a man has found his lifework. No longer does he look forth with dim surmise, wondering what may be the burden of the future. No longer does he turn to every hand in doubt as to the path he must pursue. But whether by choice, or by necessity, or by what men might call an accident, he has taken up once and for all his calling and settled down to the business of his life. When one stands amid the Alps in early morning it is often impossible to tell mountain peak from cloud. For the rising sun, touching the clouds with glory, so fashions them into fantastic pinnacles that it would take a practiced eye to tell which is cloud and which is snow-capped summit. But when noonday comes there is no longer difficulty. The clouds have separated and have disappeared, and clear and bold into the azure sky there rises up the summit of the Alps. So in our morning hour it is often hard to tell which is the cloud-capped tower and which the hill. But as the day advances and the sun mounts to noonday, that problem of the morning disappears. For clear above us rises the one summit—clear before us stretches the one work. For weal or woe we have now found our life-work, nor are we like to change it until the end.

Now with this settlement into a single task there generally comes a certain happiness. We are freed from many disquieting uncertainties that vexed us when we stood upon life's threshold. Unless a man's work be utterly abhorrent—so uncongenial as to be abhorrent—there is a quiet pleasure in those very limits that are the noticeable marks of middle age. The river no longer frets among the rocks, nor is there any glory now of dashing waterfall, but in the tranquil reaches there is a placid beauty and the suggestion of abiding peace. No more, there is an ingathering of strength—the strength that always comes of concentration. No longer does a man dissipate his powers in trying to open doors that have been barred. But knowing his work and knowing his limitations, he gives himself with his whole heart to the one thing and so is a stronger man in middle age than he was in the happy liberty of youth.

But just here arises one danger of that period—one form of "the destruction that wasteth at noonday"—and it lies in the contraction of the manhood to the one groove in which the life-work runs. The eager expectancy of youth is gone. The range of opening manhood is no more. Absorbed in the business on which his living hangs, a man contracts into a businessman. There was a day when he felt the charm of nature, but the voices of nature mean little to him now. There was a day when poetry could move him, but it is many years since he has read a poet. Strong because concentrated in his life's great work, he may be weak in that very concentration. Quietly happy because he has found his groove, he may be further from God than in his wayward youth.

There is a form of question that we often use. We ask of such and such a man, "What is he?" And you know the answer that we expect to get—he is "a teacher, a doctor, or an engineer." Now if the end for which a man was born was to be a doctor or an engineer, happy indeed would be that concentration that is so clear a feature of the noonday. But when we remember what man is, and yet shall be; when we pass in review the powers of his prime; when we think of Him in whose image man is made (which image it is the life-work to restore), do we not feel what an irony it is and what a condemnation of the noonday, that we should say of a man he *is* a draughtsman or of another he *is* an engineer? Has the promise of the morning come to this? Are these the feet that are set in a large room? (Ps. 31:8). Has all the love that blessed the years of childhood, all the preventing mercies of the spirit, all the romance and poetry of youth, all the thoughts that wandered through eternity—have all these been lavished on a man that he might become a first-rate man of business? No matter how successful a man be, if he is impoverished and contracted by success, then in the sight of God he is in peril of "the destruction that wasteth at noonday."

Faced, then, by that peril as we are, how may we reasonably hope to overcome it? One way is to have some lively interest out of the single line of the career. It may be books, it may be pictures, or it may be flowers. It may be politics, or it may be music. It does not really matter what it is, if it be an avenue into a larger world. I never knew a man who had a hobby, even if it were collecting beetles, but it tended to keep him from being a mere machine and helped him through the perils of the noonday. But there is something better than a hobby. It is the symmetry of the character of Jesus. It is the thought that there once moved on earth a Man who was perfect in the whole range of manhood. That is the value of fellowship with Christ in an age when specialism is inevitable. That is the value of fellowship with Christ in a city where men are bound to concentrate. Christ touches every string upon the harp. He vitalizes powers we would ignore. He came to give life, and to give it more abundantly, and so He saves from the destruction of the noonday.

Once more, one of the perils of the noonday is the decay and the deadening of faith. There is no period in the whole course of life in which it is so hard to walk by faith. In childhood, faith is an abiding habit. A child has a perfect genius for trusting. Dependent for everything upon the care of others, to lean on others is a sheer necessity. And so in youth is found the trustful habit—that happy reliance upon another's love—that makes the child, no matter what his faults, the type of the citizen in Jesus' kingdom. Then in old age, and when the sun is westering, faith surely must become easier again. Standing so near the margin of this world, has a man no gleams and visions of the next? So soon to make that plunge into the darkness and to leave forever the "old familiar faces," how utterly and hopelessly hardened must he be who has no thought save for the things he sees! I do not say that faith is ever easy. It is the greatest of ventures and of victories. It is the victory that overcomes the world and not to be won without a weary battle. But I do say that in youth, with its dependence, and in age, when the ship is so near the boundless deep, there is not a little to wean the heart from faithlessness, not a little that is provocative of trust.

But in middle age, as you will see at once, these helps and encouragements are wholly wanting. There is neither the stimulus of youth nor of age to lead a man to trust in the unseen. No more are we dependent upon others as we were in the happy and careless days of childhood. No more do we lean upon a father's love for the food we eat and for the clothes we wear. We are self-dependent now, and self-reliant. It is by the toil of our own hand we live. Once we depended upon another's labor, but now our livelihood hangs upon our own. Then, too, in the time of middle age there is generally a reasonable measure of good health. The days succeed each other at an even pace, and before us lies an unbroken stretch of road. Not yet do we discern the shades of evening nor feel on our cheek the chill wind of the twilight. We are far away from the brink of the beyond.

It is such facts as these that hint to us of "the destruction that wasteth at noonday." No period is so prone to materialize the spirit or to blind a man to the range of the unseen. Then first relying on our personal effort and through our effort achieving some success; then first awakening to the power of money and to all that money is able to procure; still unvisited by signs of dissolution and reasonably secure of many years, it is in middle age we run the tremendous peril of becoming worldly and materialized. Youth has its dangers, but they are those of passion, and in all passion there is something great. Very disastrous are the sins of youth, yet is there a noble lavishness about them. But the sins of middle age, though not so patent, yet in the sight of God may be more deadly, for they lead to that encrustation of the spirit that the Bible calls the hardening of the heart.

You get a company of middle-aged men together and listen to their talk about their neighbors. Is it not certain to come around to money, to their losses and to their successes and to their incomes? I do not imply that what they say is scandal. I do not even suggest it is uncharitable. I only say that they have materialized since the happy days when they were boys together. There is no time when it is harder to walk with God than on the levels of our middle age, none when it is more difficult to keep alive the vision of the eternal and unseen. For the sweet dependence of childhood is no more, and the heart has awaked to the power of the material, and not yet does the hand of death knock loudly. Brethren, who like myself have entered these mid-years, remember that Christ is praying that your faith fail not. He knows the arrow that flies in the morning; He knows the destruction that wastes at noonday. From the hard and worldly heart may Christ deliver us. May He give us the hope that is cast within the veil. Not slothful in business, but toiling at it heartily, may we endure as seeing Him who is invisible.

But not only is middle age the time when we are in peril of losing faith in God. It is also very notably the time when we are in danger of losing faith in man. The two things indeed may be said to go together, the one making way for and drawing on the other. For between faith in man and faith in God, there is ever the most vital of connections. In our days of childhood we believe in men with a romantical and splendid trust. We have not yet come into contact with them nor learned the common motives that inspire them. It is from our father we take our ideas of manhood; it is from our mother we take our ideas of womanhood. The father is ever a hero to the child, and the mother is ever worthy to be loved. Then we begin to read, and in our books we find the story of great and noble actions. We do not think of these as something rare, on the contrary we father them on every man we meet, so that all history in childish eyes is little else than a book of golden deeds. And then again, as the poet Wordsworth taught us, we clothe man in the charm of his surroundings, giving to every shepherd on the hills something of the strength of the hills on which he moves, and thinking that the life of the cottage must be beautiful because it nestles in a scene of beauty. So do we stand on the threshold of maturity, never yet brought into close touch with men, and believing in manhood with a perfect trust, yet with a trust that never has been tried.

And then with middle age comes the awaking. We see how different men are from our dreams. The vision we had of them is rudely shattered, and with the shattering there goes our faith. It may be that a young man goes to business under an employer who is a professing Christian. He may even be a pillar in the church in which the young man was baptized and trained. But in the business there are such shady tricks, such practices incompatible with honor, that in a year or two not all a father's pleading can prevail with his son to take the holy sacrament. It may be that a woman is deceived in love by someone of whom once she thought the world. It may be that a daughter lives to see that the mother whom she adored is but a worldly woman. Or it may be that, without sudden shock, we slowly discover the wheels within the wheels, the rottenness in much that is called business, the worship of money in much that is called the church, and the mean hunting after place and power that flaunts itself as patriotic politics. Every man who is the least in earnest has to pass through that disenchantment in some form. Very commonly it meets a man as youth expires and middle age begins. And it is this passage from the hopes of youth to the chilling experience of middle life that is so often attended by an eclipse of faith. Some men it makes utterly hard-hearted; others, it makes tolerantly cynical. To some it is a positive relief to find the world no better than themselves. But to all it is a deadly peril, far more insidious than sins of youth—it is "the destruction that wasteth at noonday."

There is but one help in that temptation—one help, yet it is all-sufficient. It is to remember that though He knew the worst, Christ never for an hour lost faith in man. Despised, deceived, rejected, and betrayed, still in the eyes of Christ was manhood noble. His own forsook Him on the way to Calvary, and yet He loved His own to the end. Great is our need of Christ in time of youth if we are to steer our barque amid its shoals. Great is our need of Christ when we are old if we hope to enter the eternal city. But not less great is our need of Jesus Christ in the dusty levels of our middle age if we are to be saved from that destroying angel—"the destruction that wasteth at noonday."

NOTES

The Old Man's Sermon

Charles Haddon Spurgeon (1834–1892) is undoubtedly the most famous minister of the nineteenth century. Converted in 1850, he united with the Baptists and soon began to preach in various places. He became pastor of the Baptist church in Waterbeach, England, in 1851, and three years later he was called to the decaying Park Street Church, London. Within a short time the work began to prosper, a new church was built and dedicated in 1861, and Spurgeon became London's most popular preacher. In 1855, he began to publish his sermons weekly; today they make up the fifty-seven volumes of *The Metropolitan Tabernacle Pulpit*. He founded a pastor's college and several orphanages.

This sermon was taken from *The Metropolitan Tabernacle Pulpit,* volume 21.

Charles Haddon Spurgeon

10

THE OLD MAN'S SERMON

O God, thou hast taught me from my youth: and hitherto
have I declared thy wondrous works. Now also when I
am old and grayheaded, O God, forsake me not; until I
have shewed thy strength unto this generation, and thy
power to every one that is to come (Psalm 71:17–18).

I EXPECT DURING THE present week to have the pleasure of
preaching at Kettering to celebrate the centenary of the
ministry in that place of Mr. Toller and his father. My
esteemed friend Mr. Toller has for about fifty-five years
proclaimed the Gospel of the grace of God to the same
people, and with the forty-five years of his father's
previous pastorate the century is completed. Having this
very pleasant task before me, I have been led to consider
the subject of old age, especially the old age of believers.
I have concluded that *"the reminiscences of an old man"*
would furnish us a suitable topic for this morning's
discourse. I was the more led to choose the subject
because on Sabbath week the children and young people
will have a claim upon the preacher, since that day has
been selected by the Sunday School Union for special
prayer. To balance accounts, let us give this morning's
service to our grave and reverend seniors.

David has here spoken as an aged man, and what he
has said has been echoed by thousands of venerable believers. His experience of the past, his prayer for the
present, and his aspiration for the future have all occurred to others who are his equals in years. And those
of us who are in middle life will before long be glad to
say "Amen" thereto. "O God, thou hast taught me from
my youth: and hitherto have I declared thy wondrous
works. Now also when I am old and grayheaded, O God,
forsake me not." David in this passage may be regarded
as the model of an aged believer converted in early life.

131

We feel quite safe in taking all his expressions and putting them into the mouths of veteran soldiers of the Cross.

David's Scholarship

The first thing we shall dwell upon this morning will be scholarship, *or a good beginning.* "God, thou hast taught me from my youth." *The psalmist was an instructed believer.* He had not merely been saved, but taught: conversion had led to instruction. I call the attention of all young Christians to this. How desirable it is not merely that you should be forgiven your sins and justified by faith in Christ Jesus, and that your hearts should be renewed by the operations of the Holy Spirit, but that you should go to school to Jesus, take His yoke upon you, and learn of Him. Do you not know that this is the good part that Mary chose, and which the Lord declared should not be taken away from her? She chose to sit at His feet to learn of Him. Do not suppose that to be saved from hell is everything; you need also to be instructed in righteousness. If you seek to know the Lord more and more, it will save you from a thousand snares, cause you to grow in grace, and enable you to be useful. That will be a fruitful old age that was preceded by an instructed youth. We ought to know the truth and understand it, for if we do not, we shall always be weak in the faith. That David was exceedingly well instructed is clear from his psalms, which contain a mine of doctrine and a wealth of experience never surpassed even by other inspired writings. If one had no other book than the Psalms to study, he might, by the blessing of God's Spirit, become one of the wisest of men. Aim, then, my friends to be disciples now that in your old age you may look back with joy on the days spent in heavenly learning.

All his instruction the psalmist traced to his God. "O God, thou hast taught me." He had entered Christ's College as a scholar. Most wisely had he chosen to learn of Him who has infinite wisdom to impart, and divine skill in communicating it. The Lord not only endeavors to teach, but He does do so. He knows how to make His children learn, for He speaks to the heart and teaches us to profit. "O God, thou hast taught me." What a blessed thing it is when we are fully convinced by the Holy Spirit that to learn anything aright we must be taught of God. Too many appear to fancy that everything they need to know they can discover for themselves; they can work it out by their own thoughts. At any rate, the profound learning of their favorite authors will carry them through. You who have grown gray in your Master's service, I am sure you have learned to mistrust your own understanding and are glad to receive the kingdom of heaven as a little child. You know by experience that all you have ever learned apart from God has been a lesson of sorrow or of folly. You have obtained no true light except from the great Father of lights. No heavenly truths are learned aright until by the Holy Spirit they are burned into the soul. Blessed are those who have gone to school to such a Master, they shall be among the wise who shall shine as the brightness of the firmament.

The Lord had taught David in part by His Word, for we find David delighting in the Scriptures and meditating in them both day and night. He taught him also by his ministers. He gathered no little instruction from Samuel and learned some pointed lessons from Nathan, while Gad, the king's seer, no doubt, also ministered to his building up. God's children are willing to be taught by God's servants. He had also been instructed by the Holy Spirit. Many a precious truth had been communicated to him in the quiet of the sheep hills or in the solitary caverns of the hills. Even when he had become a king he was awakened in the night watches that he might hear the voice of the Lord his God. Moreover, the Lord taught him by providence. He learned much from his shepherd's crook, much from his sling and stone, much from the hatred of Saul, much from the love of Jonathan. He must have learned much afterward of his own heart from his own trials, follies, and sins. He must have seen much of man's worthlessness from the ingratitude of Absalom, the treachery of Ahithophel, the brutality of Joab, and the blasphemy of Shimei. His whole life was a course of education. Whether he stood on the hill Mizar or traversed the valley of Baca, whether he exulted in green pastures or sunk in the depths where all God's waves and billows went over him, whether he sang a hallelujah or chanted a *miserere,* everything was training him for a yet nobler existence. Hence he could say to the most High, "Thou hast taught me."

O beloved Christian friends, in looking back can you not see how everything has been instructive to you when you have been willing to learn? What a school have some of us passed through, a school of trial and a school of love. We have sat on the hard form of discipline, and we have felt the rod of correction. On the other hand our eyes have sparkled with delight as we have studied the illuminated book of fellowship and peered into the secret of the Lord, which is with them that fear Him. To us has been fulfilled that ancient covenant promise, "all thy children shall be taught of the LORD."

David also had the privilege of beginning early. "O God, thou hast taught me from my youth." I was a scholar in Your infant class. I was put to You to learn my letters. When I learned to spell out Your name as my Savior and Father, it was Your grace that taught it to me. All true learning begins at Christ's feet, and it is well to be there in our boyhood. If you would be a good scholar you must be a young scholar. David felt that he needed to be instructed of God from his youth, for in one of his psalms he says, "Remember not the sins of my youth, and my former transgressions." Even pious David had sins of his youth to mourn over and, therefore, needed as well as others to learn the way of holiness when young. The dire necessity that the foolishness of nature has laid upon us from our earliest days is met by early grace. My aged brethren and sisters, I would urge you at this moment to bless the Lord for the grace that in early days saved many of you from falling into grievous sin.

The sin that the psalmist mourned over he was enabled by divine teaching to master. He says himself, "Wherewithal shall a young man cleanse his way? By taking heed thereto according to thy word," and so David had done. Hence his early life was marked by great purity and simplicity of character because he had been so well taught of God. Specially had he been taught to *trust* his God, for in the fifth verse of this psalm he says, "Thou art my hope, O LORD God, thou art my trust from my youth." Being so taught he had practically proved his faith, for while he was yet in his youth he smote the uncircumcised Philistine and in the name of God delivered Israel. Blessed is that young man who practically shows by daring deeds that he is a disciple of Jesus. Blessed is that old man who in looking back confesses that he needed teaching from his youth up, but also rejoices that he received instruction from the Lord and was led into the way of righteousness.

Further, notice David tells us *he kept to his studies.* He says, "God, thou hast taught me *from* my youth," which implies that God had continued to teach him—and so indeed He had. The learner had not sought another school, nor had the Master turned off His pupil. Some make slight progress because they seem to begin well but afterward turn aside to folly. They profess to be taught of God at one time, but they grow weary of the plain Gospel of Jesus and resort to heresy-mongers and inventors of strange doctrines. Good is it for the heart to be established in the truth and to yield itself to no teacher but the Lord. Venerable brother and sister, I hope you can say, "O God, You have taught me from my youth. I have not bowed my soul to every wind of doctrine and made myself as the bulrush, which yields to every passing breath of air. But I have been steadfast, unmovable, holding fast the word of truth."

It is equally clear that *he was still learning.* The oldest saint still goes to school to the Lord Jesus. Oh, how little we know when we know most. The wisest saints are those who most readily confess their folly. The man who knows everything is the man who knows nothing. The man who cannot learn any more is the man who has never learned anything aright. To know Christ and the power of His resurrection creates an insatiable thirst after a still closer acquaintance with Him. Our eager desire is yet more fully "to know him."

I half wish that I could leave the pulpit and that some venerable brother could come forward and tell you how God began with him, and repeat the first lessons that he learned. I would like to hear him tell how God has had patience with him and has taught him still. I would like to hear how sometimes he has had to smart under the rod before he could be made to learn at all, and yet the Lord has been gentle with him. I would like "such an one as Paul the aged" to tell you how by everything that has happened, bad and good, bright and dark, his education has been carried on. I would like him to tell you how glad he is to continue to be a learner, though now so far advanced in life. The best instructed of our elder brethren and sisters are those who most earnestly cry, "What I know not teach thou me," and "Open thou mine eyes, that I may behold wondrous things out of thy law." Though my venerable friend has earned to himself a good degree, he still keeps to his old book and his old Master. Though now able to teach others also, he is nonetheless a disciple, sitting at the feet of Jesus. Yes, he is all the more teachable because of what he already knows.

Thus, friends, we have seen that the model of aged believers is an instructed saint who owes all he knows to divine teaching. He began to learn early and has persevered in his sacred studies even to this day.

> 'Twas thine, O Lord, to train and try
>   My spirit from my youth;
> And to this hour I glorify
>   The wonders of thy truth.

David's Occupation

His scholarship was a good beginning; his occupation was *a good continuance*—"Hitherto have I declared thy wondrous works." This was David's chief employment. It is true he had other work to do, for he was at first a shepherd. He then became a royal harper, afterward grew into a warrior, and at last climbed to a throne. Still his life's main bent and object was to magnify the Lord by declaring His wondrous works. You and I have each one our calling. If it be a lawful calling let us abide in it, and let us not dream that it would honor God for us to leave our daily occupations upon pretense of serving Him in a more spiritual way by living upon other people. Still our earthly vocation is but the shell of our heavenly calling, which is the kernel of our life's pursuit. Our temporal business must be subservient to our spiritual business, and we must declare the glory of God in some way or other.

David magnified the Lord by his psalms. How sweetly has he therein declared God's ways of mercy and of faithfulness! He glorified God by his life, especially by those heroic deeds that made all Israel know the mighty works that God could do by a feeble but trustful man. He no doubt often declared the wondrous works of God in private converse with believers and unbelievers by narrating his personal experience of the Lord's mercies. You and I, if we have been to God's school, must follow the same occupation. Some of us can preach, let us be diligent in it. Others of you teach in the school. I beseech you put your whole hearts into that blessed work. All of you can by written letters or private conversation, and especially by consistent lives, declare the wondrous works of God and make men know the glories of the God of grace. Let us be eager in this sacred work. Men and women do not care to know their God, but we must not allow them to be ignorant. Tell them of that love of His against which they daily offend and of His readiness to forgive their provocations. Publish and proclaim salvation by grace. It is sweet in old age to remember that you did this.

Notice here, dear friends, that *David had chosen a divine subject.* "Hitherto have I declared thy wondrous works." *God's* works he had declared, not man's. He had not talked of what man could do or had done. Note verse sixteen: "I will make mention of thy righteousness, even of thine only." Neither the virtues of saints, nor the prerogatives of priests, nor the infallibility of pontiffs, nor anything of the sort had degraded the psalmist's lips. But those lips had reserved themselves for the glory of God alone. "My tongue also shall talk of thy righteousness all the day long."

We ought to speak of what God has done in creation, providence, and grace. We should especially point out the marvelous nature of those works, for there is a wonder about them all. Truly, friends, here is a great subject for us—the wonders of electing love, the wonders of redeeming grace, the wonders of the Holy Spirit's converting power, the wonders of sanctification, the wonders of sin conquered and of grace implanted. Such wonders never cease. Wonders of grace to God belong. It should be your business and mine, in the spirit of holy reverence, to tell out to others what God has done that we may set them wondering and adoring too.

David had a blessed subject, a subject of which the main point was the blending of righteousness with salvation. Did you notice the fifteenth verse, "My mouth shall show forth thy righteousness and thy salvation all the day"? That is the great Christian doctrine—*medulla theologiæ,* the very pith and marrow of theology—the atonement in which grace and justice unite in the sacrifice of Jesus. O beloved, I could wish to have no other subject to speak upon, and to have my tongue touched with a live coal from off the altar to preach of substitution only. I desire to speak of it first and foremost and beyond all else. I would show forth daily how God is just, and yet the Justifier of him that believes in Jesus. I would show forth how He smites for sin, and yet smites not the sinner. I would show forth how He is severe, relaxing none of the penalty, yet laying none of the penalty upon the guilty because the Guiltless One has borne it all. Make it, dear friends, the occupation of your lives to instruct people in this saving truth; teach them this if nothing else. If there are some doctrines you cannot understand, yet get a grip of this. If some are too high for you, yet let this be your daily theme—Christ crucified, at whose Cross righteousness and peace have kissed each other. This was David's occupation. My aged friends in Christ, this has been your occupation also, and you do not regret it. You only wish you had been more diligent in it.

Now notice that while David's subject was divine, it

had also been *uniform*. He says, *"Hitherto* have I declared thy wondrous works." It is a sad thing when a good man turns aside to error, even if it be but for a little season. Some ministers have preached motley. I would think they themselves do not know what they have taught, for they have gone from one line of thought to another, and contradicted themselves over and over again. Beware of being men and women given to change, ready to catch every new disease. I confess I feel an admiration for a man who can say, "What I taught in my youth I teach in my old age. That which was my hope and confidence when first the Spirit of God opened my mouth, that and no other is my hope and confidence still." As men and women grow in years they ought to think more deeply, to understand more clearly, and to speak with greater confidence. It is their wisdom to correct many errors of detail that occurred through the immaturity of their early days. But still it is a great thing to hold fundamental truth from the very first. There are not two Christs nor two Gospels. If there be another gospel, it is not another, but there be some that trouble us. Oh, my friend, if the Lord has taught you from your youth, abide in that which you have learned, hold to it now that your hair is gray. Let us see that "the Old Guard dies but never surrenders." Even we, who are younger than you are, have resolved to abide in the grand old truth. Our flag was nailed to the mast long ago; surely the veterans will say the same. All my salvation and all my desire are centered in the covenant of grace and the Gospel of redemption by the blood of Jesus. As for novelties of doctrine, I have one answer for them all:

> Should all the forms which men devise
> Assault my faith with treacherous art,
> I'd call them vanity and lies,
> And bind the gospel to my heart.

That is a good word of permanence—*hitherto*—"hitherto have I declared thy wondrous works." Hitherto also have our aged fathers came, holding still the things most surely believed among us.

But, dear friends, notice that *the style that David used was very commendable.* "Hitherto have I *declared,*" says he. Now by declaration I understand something positive, plain, and personal. David's teaching about his God had not been with an "if" and a "but" and a "maybe," but it had been "Thus and thus, saith the Lord." He had declared the truth openly. His teaching had not been misty and foggy, so that his people could make what they liked out of it according to their tastes. Neither had it been mystical, metaphysical, transcendental, and philosophic, but he had declared it, cleared it, explained it, and brought it into prominent notice, so that he who ran might read it. He had also declared it as known to himself and certified by his own experience. It is a blessed thing to give a personal tinge to our testimony by saying, "Thus and thus have I experienced, and so has the Lord dealt with me." Herein will lie much of the interest of our testimony. Dear friend, you who have attained to a ripe old age, I trust you are able in looking back to say, "Yes, I have spoken honestly for God from my inmost heart. Therefore I have spoken with decision, proving by my personal experience the truth of the divine promises. God has always been true to me, and though some may think me an egotist I can bear the censure, for I am unable to restrain myself from uttering my grateful acknowledgments. Surely if I did not speak the stones would cry out. I must proclaim the faithfulness of the living God."

David's style had in it very much of holy awe and loving devotion, for he says, "thy *wondrous* works," which shows that he himself had wondered while he spoke. I like to hear a good man talk of God's love, feeling it to be too deep for him. To hear a good man speaking of it with tears, as though it overcame him; telling his tale as though it were more marvelous to him than he could make it appear to his hearers. David had done his work in the spirit of adoring wonder and grateful love. He had ever before him this one object, to make God great in men's thoughts. May I ask you who are getting on in years, are you making this your one occupation? And, if you happen to be teachers or preachers, do you teach the salvation of God with the sole aim of glorifying God? Oh, it must come to this, for all divine service that is not rendered with this motive is unacceptable and idle work. If we could preach with the tongues of men and of angels so as to surpass Apollos, if our object were to shine in the eyes of men, our preaching would be as sounding brass or a tinkling cymbal. If there be any mixture in the motive, dead flies are in the ointment of the apothecary, and it gives forth an ill savor. But if this be our one sole desire, to glorify God by making men see what a great and blessed God he is, our labor will be as the incense upon the golden altar. Upon such service we shall be able to look back in our old age with thankfulness. How is it with you, my brother, my sister, in reviewing the past? And how are matters with you who are in the prime of your strength—are you about your Father's business and living for God in all that you do? Oh, then, happy shall you be when gray hairs shall adorn your heads with a crown of glory. The silver light shall not rest on your heads only, but shall cast its sheen of gladness upon your hearts also as you remember that hitherto you have declared His wondrous works.

David's Prayer

Thus I pass on to the third thing in the text, namely, his prayer, which was *a good omen—"Now also when I am old and grayheaded, O God, forsake me not."* What a plaintive prayer it is. It shows you that David was not ashamed of *his former reliance.*

He felt that he should not have come so far if God had not led him. He saw his absolute dependence upon God in the past, the necessity that had always existed for his entire reliance on the divine omnipotence. I hope that from our youth we have known the necessity of dependence upon God, but I am certain that dependence is a growing feeling. Growing Christians think themselves nothing; full-grown Christians think themselves less than nothing. Good men are like ships, the fuller they are the lower they sink in the stream. The more grace a

man has the more he complains of his want of grace.
Grace is not a kind of food that creates a sense of fullness. But as I have heard of some meats that you can
eat them until you are hungry, so it is with grace—the
more you receive the more you long for. David knew the
secret springs from which all his blessings had flowed.
He pleads with the Lord never to stop the divine fountain of all-sufficiency, or he must faint and die.

This proves, dear friends, that David did not imagine
that past grace could suffice for the present. Past experience is like the old manna, it breeds worms and stinks
if it be relied upon. The moment a man begins to pride
himself on the grace he used to have six years ago, you
may depend upon it that he has very little now. We want
new grace every day. The presence of God with me yesterday will not suffice for the present moment. I must
have grace now. David acknowledged his *present dependence,* and it was wise to do so. Men always stumble
when they try to walk with their eyes turned behind
them. It is very remarkable that all the falls, as far as I
remember, recorded in Scripture are those of old men.
This should be a great warning to us who think we are
getting wise and experienced. Lot, Judah, Eli, Solomon,
and Asa were all advanced in years when they were
found faulty before the Lord. Cool passions are no guar-
antees against fiery sins, unless grace has cooled them
rather than decay of nature. There was great need for
David to say, "O God, forsake me not," and his own case
proved it. I have heard said by those who drive much,
that horses fall more often at the bottom of the hill than
anywhere else. Where the driver thinks he need not hold
them up any longer, down they go. Thus many men have
borne temptation bravely for years. But just when the
trial was over and we reckoned that they were safe, they
turned aside to crooked ways and grieved the Lord. You
are greatly surprised. You would have believed it of anybody sooner than of them, but so it is. Take this, then,
as a caution, lest we spoil a lifelong reputation by one
wretched act of sin. My very heart cries, "O God, forsake
me not."

The psalmist saw that many enemies were watching him, and therefore he pleaded, "Forsake me not." He had many temptations to grow weary in his Master's service, and he prayed, "Forsake me not." He felt also the natural decay of his physical force, and he cried, "My strength faileth." Therefore he pleaded, "Forsake me not."

> With years oppressed, with sorrows worn,
> Dejected, harassed, sick, forlorn,
>   To thee, O God, I pray;
> To thee my withered hands arise,
> To thee I lift these failing eyes;
>   Oh, cast me not away!

The psalmist by this prayer confessed *his undeservingness*. He felt that for his sins God might well leave him. Hence that prayer in the fifty-first Psalm, "Cast me not away from thy presence; take not thy Holy Spirit from me." But he humbly resolved not to be deserted; he could not bear it. He held his God with eagerness and cried in agony, "O God, forsake me not." His heart was desperately set upon holding to his one hope and consolation, and so he pleaded as one who pleads for life itself.

You now have the prayer before you. Do you think the Lord will answer it? You who are feeling your strength fail through old age have been praying, "O God, forsake me not." What do you think; will the Lord answer your prayer? Aye, that he will! It is not possible for Him to do otherwise. Do you think it is like our Lord to leave a man because he is growing old? Would any of us do it? Son, would you cast off your father because he totters about the house? Brother, would you leave your elder brother because he is now aged and infirm? Do we any of us, as long as we have human hearts in our bosom, pitilessly desert the aged? Oh no, and God is far better than we are. He will not despise His worn-out servants. The feeble moanings of the most afflicted and infirm are heard by Him, not with weariness, but with pity. Do you think the Lord will turn off His old servants? Would you do so? Among men it is common enough to leave poor old people to shift for themselves. The soldier who has spent the prime of his life in his country's service has been left to beg by the roadside or to die of want. Even the saviors of a nation have been suffered in their old age to pine in penury. How often have kings and princes cast off their most faithful servants and left them naked to their enemies! When time has wrinkled the handsome face and bowed the erect figure, the old man has no longer found a place in the throng of courtiers. But the Lord deals not so. The King of kings casts not off His veteran soldiers, nor His old courtiers, but He indulges them with peculiar favors. We have a proverb that old wine and old friends are best, and truly we need not look far to see that the oldest saints are frequently the best esteemed by the Lord. He did not forsake Abraham when he was well stricken in years, nor Isaac when he was blind, nor Jacob when he worshiped upon the top of his staff.

Who among us would turn off an old servant? Some skinflints who have no sense of shame might do so, but they are a disgrace to their kind. I know my Lord and Master will never act as they do, for He is love and His mercy endures forever. If He has blessed us in youth and middle life, He will not change His ways and desert us in our declining days. No, blessed be His name, at eventide it will be light and He will show Himself more tender than ever to us. For he has said, "Even to old age I am he, and even to hoary hairs will I carry you: I have made, and I will bear; even I will carry, and will deliver you."

No, my friends, Jesus will not forget his old Barzillais. Nor, though like Peter, others should gird us and take us whither we would not, He will not turn away His face from us, but will love us to the end.

Why, friends, if the Lord had meant to have cast us off would He not have done so long ago? If He wanted occasion for discharging us from His service, has He not had plenty? My Lord has had reason enough to send me packing hundreds of times if He had willed to do so. He has not waited all these years to pick a quarrel with you at the last, I am sure, for He might have justly removed you from His household years ago. If He had meant to destroy you, would He have shown you such things as He has done? If He meant to leave you, would He not have left you in your troubles twenty years ago? He has spent so much patience and pains and trouble over you that He surely means to go through with it. Why should He not? Has He begun to build and is He not able to finish? Trembling friend, remember that your vessel has been steered across the ocean of life for seventy years. Surely you can trust the Lord to pilot you for the few years that remain? Did you say that you are nearly eighty, and do you still doubt your God? How long do you expect to live? Another ten years? Cannot you trust Him for that? Why, you will not be here so long as that, in all probability. Since the Lord has been good to you so long, do you doubt now? Oh, do not so. It is almost Saturday night, the week's work is nearly done, and you will soon enjoy the everlasting Sabbath. Can you not rely upon your God until the day break and the shadows flee away. "Ah," say you, "you are only a young man; it is very well for you to talk." I know it; I know it. Yet I believe that when I grow old I shall be able to talk as I do now, and even more confidently, for I trust I shall then be able to say, "He who taught me from my youth and kept me to this day, will not now let me go." Oh, my friend, though you cried in prayer, "God, forsake me not," do not sink so low as to imagine that He can forsake you. To imagine that would be to mistrust His royal Word wherein He said, "I will never leave thee nor forsake thee."

David's Wish

Our last point is this, here is his wish, or *a good ending*. "Forsake me not *till I have shewed thy strength unto this generation and thy power to every one that is to come*." He had spent a lifetime in declaring God's Gospel, but he wanted to do it once more. Aged saints are loth to cease from active service. Many of them are like old John Newton who, when he was too feeble to walk up the pulpit stairs of St. Mary Woolnoth parish church, was carried up to his place and preached on still. His friends said,

"Really, Mr. Newton, you are so feeble, you ought to give over." He said, "What? Shall the old African blasphemer ever leave off preaching the grace of his Master as long as there is breath in his body? No, never." It is harder work to leave off than to go on, for the love of Christ constrains us still and burns with young flame in an aged heart. So here the good man pines to show forth once more God's strength. I think I hear somebody say to the aged man, "You are very unfit to show forth God's strength, for by reason of years your strength is failing." But such a speech would be foolish, for the very man to show forth the Lord's strength is the man who has none of his own. It is no small thing to be in a condition to need great help, and so to be fitted to receive it and qualified to illustrate what great things divine power can accomplish. My aged friend, your weakness will serve as a foil to set forth the brightness of divine strength. The "old man eloquent" feels that if he could bear one more testimony everybody would know it was not the strength of his natural spirit or his fine juvenile constitution that upheld him. If he spoke up for his Maker all men would say, "That feeble old man who testified so bravely for his Lord is himself the best of all testimonies to the power of divine grace, for we see how it strengthens him."

Moreover, he thought that if he witnessed for his Lord the young people would note the strength of divine grace, which could last out so many years. They would see that many waters could not quench love, neither could the floods drown it. They would see the strength of God's pardoning mercy in blotting out his sins so long, and the power of God's faithfulness in remaining true to His servant, even to the end. Because of all this he eagerly desired to bear one more testimony.

And, do you notice the congregation he wished to address. He would testify to the generation that was growing up around him. He wished to make known God's power to his immediate neighbors and to their children so that the light might be handed on to other generations. This should be on the mind of all who are going off the stage of action. They should think of those who are to come after them, pray for them, and help them. The aged man's thoughts should be fixed upon the spiritual legacies that he will leave. As good old Jacob gathered up his feet in the bed and then divided his blessing among his sons, so should the venerable believer distribute benedictions. Your work is almost done; it only remains to leave behind you a monument by which you may be remembered. Marble and brass will perish, but truth will remain—set up a memorial of faithful testimony. Not much longer will you mingle with the sons of men. Your seat will be empty here, and the place that knows you today will know you no more. Hand on, then, the blessed treasure of the Gospel. You die, but the cause of God must not. Speak now, so that when you are gone it may be said of you, "He being dead yet speaketh." Call your children and your grandchildren together and tell them what a good God you have served. If you have no such dear ones, speak to your neighbors and your friends, or write it down that other eyes may read it when yours are glazed in death. Reach out your hand to the ages yet to come and present them with the pearl of great price. Pray God to enable you to set your mark upon the coming generation, and then set about winning youth to Jesus by a cheerful, bold, unhesitating witness to His love and power. Willing to go we all ought to be, but we ought scarcely to desire departure until we have seen the interests of the cause of God secured for coming time. If there is one more soul to be saved, one more heart to be comforted, one more jewel to be gathered for the Redeemer's crown, you will say, dear friend, I am sure, "Let me wait until my full day's work is done."

> Happy if with my latest breath
> I may but lisp thy name,
> Preach thee to all, and say in death,
> "Behold, behold the Lamb!"

With the last practical thought I send away my venerable brethren and sisters, asking them to take care that their eventide shall be made to glow with the special light of usefulness by their abundant witness-bearing. I would urge the Lord's veterans to yet more valorous deeds. If, like David, you have slain the lion and the bear and the Philistine when you were young, up man, and do another deed of daring, for the Lord lives still, and His people have need of you. Though your joints are rather rusty and your limbs can hardly bear you to the battlefield, yet limp to the conflict, for the lame take the prey. He who helped you when you were but a youth and ruddy, will help you now though you are old and infirm. Who knows what you may do yet! One of the finest paintings I ever saw to move one's soul was the picture of old Dandolo, the Doge of Venice, leading the way in an attack at sea upon the enemies of the Republic. He was far past the usual age of man and blind. Yet, when the efforts of others failed to save his country, he became the leader and was the first to board the ships of the enemy. The young men felt that they could not hold back when they saw the heroic conduct of the blind, gray-bearded man. His brave example seemed to say, "Soldiers of Venice, will you ever turn your backs?" The response was worthy of the challenge. Oh, my honored brethren and sisters, reverend for your years, show us your metal. Let the young ones see how victories are won. Quit yourselves like men, and let us see how he who is washed in the blood would not hesitate to shed his own blood in the Redeemer's cause. Your zeal will stimulate us, your courage nerve us, and we, too, will be valiant for the Lord God of Israel. So may God's Spirit work in you and in us. Amen.

NOTES

"Passing on the Torch"

Archibald Thomas Robertson (1863–1934) was
converted to Christ when thirteen and licensed to preach
when eighteen. He was ordained in 1888 but had to
resign a few months later because of ill health. That same
year, he married the daughter of John A. Broadus, noted
homiletics professor at Southern Baptist Seminary in
Louisville, and served as Broadus's assistant until
Broadus died in 1895. Robertson was named Professor
of New Testament Interpretation, a position he held until
his death in 1934. The author of forty-five books, all of
them scholarly, he is best known for his monumental *A
Grammar of the Greek New Testament* and his six-
volume *Word Pictures in the Greek New Testament*. He
was an effective preacher who used his scholarship
wisely and never paraded it in the pulpit.

This sermon was taken from *Passing on the Torch,*
published in 1934 by Fleming H. Revell.

Archibald Thomas Robertson

11

"PASSING ON THE TORCH"

For which reason I am reminding thee to keep blazing the gift of God. . . . Deposit these with reliable men who will be able to teach others also (2 Timothy 1:6; 2:2).

THE TITLE FOR THIS sermon is obtained by combining the metaphor of rekindling the spark *(anazōpurein)* in 2 Timothy 1:6 with the second verse of the second chapter when Paul exhorts Timothy to "deposit" what he had heard from him with reliable men who will be able to teach others also. Timothy with his own fire blazing is to set fire to others who will pass on the torch. Ordinarily we are not to mix metaphors or to combine detached verses of Scripture. One who is skillful at such jugglery with texts can prove any proposition that he wishes. An obvious illustration is this: "Judas went and hanged himself. Go thou and do likewise. And what thou doest, do quickly." But in this instance the result is wholly in accord with the tenor of 2 Timothy. Paul is greatly concerned that Timothy shall be able to propagate the Gospel message effectively after Paul himself is gone.

The metaphor in *anazōpurein* is a graphic one. The present active infinitive expresses linear or continual action. It is a double compound that occurs in the vernacular papyri, but only here in the New Testament. *Pur* is fire, *zōo* is alive, and *ana* means again. The substantive *zōpuron* (a live fire) occurs either for embers (live coals) or for a pair of bellows with which to blow into flame the live coals. So then Paul is here urging Timothy not to let the fire from God in his soul go out, but to fan it into flame. The gift of God is in Timothy, Paul says, but it is up to Timothy to blow it into a blaze. This simple fact helps explain why some men of smaller gifts may make a bigger blaze by blowing harder and longer. In

151

1 Thessalonians 5:19 Paul employs the same metaphor of fire in relation to the Holy Spirit: "Quench not the Spirit." That is a habit that will put the fire out in any life. Jesus Himself applied the figure of fire to His own ministry (Luke 12:49): "I came to cast fire upon the earth, and what do I wish if it is already kindled" (or, How I wish that it were already kindled). Timothy is to keep his own fire going. We became familiar with this thought during the World War when everybody was singing "Keep the Home Fires Burning."

Five words can be used to bring out Paul's ideas on this subject in these passages:

Inheritance

Paul is rich in his spiritual inheritance in God whom he has been serving from his forefathers. He once had great pride in his Jewish, not to say Pharisaic, ancestry and environment, and could boast of it on occasion, though a foolish thing to do as he knew (2 Cor. 11:22ff.). Now as a Christian, Paul no longer glories in such things, which are mere refuse in comparison with what Jesus offers (Phil. 3:5–11). But Paul still feels gratitude to God for the pious ancestry that was his and reminds Timothy, too, of his debt to his mother Eunice and to his grandmother Lois. Timothy's tears remind Paul of his emotional nature and tender regard for the two women who shaped his training. Timothy's father was a Greek and so out of this noble line of faith in God (Acts 16:1). One may cherish the hope that Timothy was able to win his own father to faith in Christ. It is impossible to exaggerate the value of a pious heritage such as both Paul and Timothy possessed.

Only we must bear in mind that genuine faith such as Timothy had (unhypocritical faith) is a personal matter and not a mere matter of inheritance, or of heredity, to use the scientific term. That was and is a common fallacy in religion. John the Baptist had to warn the Pharisees and Sadducees who came to his baptism against saying within themselves: "We have Abraham as our father" (Matt. 3:9; Luke 3:8) and therefore need no personal change in heart or life. The Jews held that Abraham possessed a superfluity of merit that overflowed to all of his descendants. That is a heresy none too rare today with husbands who serve God by proxy. That is, the wife attends church and gives money from the husband while he abstains from outward service to Christ. He enjoys his own pleasures and actually has a dim hope of eternal life on the ground of his wife's piety. Such husbands may go to heaven by proxy also. The wife will go to heaven while the husband goes elsewhere.

And yet the child of pious parents does have a better chance of being saved than the children of worldly people and of the slums. It is possible, most assuredly, for men and women of evil ancestry and wicked associations to be converted, radically and completely changed from darkness to light and life. That miracle is one of the continual proofs of the reality and the power of Christianity. We know that Christ is alive today because He does lift men and women out of the gutter and set them upon their feet. This is a blessed and a glorious fact and a ground for gratitude. And yet, one who, like Paul and Timothy, comes to Christ out of a Christian home has special reason for gratitude to God for His manifold mercies, for hallowed memories of pious loved ones, for being started when young to walk in the way of life, for the chance of having a long life of Christian growth and service, for the many years of fellowship with Jesus Christ here.

To be sure, not all children from pious homes respond to their environment. Some react in the other direction and rebel against a mother's prayers and a father's counsel, to show their independence. That is true, but by no means so common as people imagine. There is a popular superstition, sometimes amounting to prejudice, that preachers' sons are worse than those of men of other callings. The stirring examples of such derelicts are allowed to give color to the whole group. Examination of *Who's Who* has revealed the fact that there are sixteen times as many names of preachers' sons and daughters in that list of notables as there should be in proportion to the number from other callings in life. The child of devout parents has all the advantages in the race for a useful career.

It is a high and holy privilege for a father or mother to lead the child to trust in Christ, one that should be cherished and practiced. That is one of life's chief joys as many can testify. Occasionally one finds a father, and even a mother or grandmother, who opposes the child's taking a stand for Christ until he is some fifteen years of age. That is a terrible, and often fatal, blunder. The child should be allowed and encouraged to give his heart to Christ. Paul reminds Timothy that such an inheritance of faith calls for courage, not cowardice, on his part.

Preparedness

Timothy was blessed in his teachers (his mother and his grandmother) who had taught him "the sacred writings." He should never forget that fact nor what he had learned from them. In fact, Timothy himself, even as a boy, on occasion had to take his father's place (he being a Greek) and recite the Scriptures himself (acting thus as head of the family). Many a man has stored away in his mind the Scriptures committed to memory when a child. They are still the portions best known and most prized and easiest to use against the tempter, or to console or strengthen oneself in trouble. This process began with Timothy "from a babe," that is, from his childhood.

It is one of the tragedies of modern life that so many children are not taught any part of the Bible at home. Some homes, alas, have no Bible. Others have a copy, but neglect it. The Bible is still the best seller of all books. But all too many fail to read it themselves, and still more neglect to teach it to their children. Family prayers are no longer common, and our complicated way of living works a hardship on the child. Many public schools are not allowed to have daily readings from the Bible. The Sunday school lessons remain the only help for many, but the lessons are brief and only once a week. The Daily Vacation Bible School supplies a real need in many communities. The preaching service, unfortunately, is not largely attended by the children, and even so the preacher does not always open the Scriptures in a helpful manner for them.

But the Scriptures are powerful today, as of old, and able to make children and men wise to salvation through faith in Christ Jesus. It is not bibliolatry that Paul here commands, but the use of the Scriptures to turn one to faith in Christ Jesus. He alone is the Savior from sin. There is no magic or charm in the Scriptures like an amulet that some superstitious people wear. The Pharisees took scraps of the Old Testament and put them in a box and wore them as "phylacteries" (guards to ward off evil) on the arm or the forehead. The Word of God is a lamp to the feet only when it has illumined the heart and life. "All Scripture is God-breathed and useful for teaching, for reproof, for setting one straight, for training in righteousness." Each item here can be verified in the life of each of us, if he will only give it a chance.

Paul gives the purpose in this use of the Scriptures as a preparation for service, "that the man of God may be fully equipped" *(artios,* an old and common adjective from *arō* to fit, to equip). No one is "fitted" for service without adequate knowledge of the Scriptures. Inefficiency among servants of Christ, preachers included, is largely due to ignorance of the Scriptures. The man who has this equipment is "completely furnished unto every good work." As a boy in Statesville, North Carolina, about 1876, I used to see the horses step promptly to the fire engine when the clock struck twelve, and almost instantly dash off with the engine as soon as the harness was clamped upon them. They were trained for service.

If only church members were trained in the Scriptures, they would as readily respond to every call for service at church or elsewhere—in attendance, in offerings, in soulwinning. There is a mighty army of nominal Christians in the world, but the most of them cannot be counted on for actual response to any call for action. They are not trained in the Scriptures. They feel no sense of responsibility for the work and on-going of the kingdom of God or even of the local church to which they belong.

They do not give themselves the proper environment, to use another scientific term, for proper functioning. They wither and dry up and drop away for lack of nourishment. They are not fed on the Word of life, but fill their minds and hearts wholly on the movies, the sex magazines and novels, the current whirl in the daily papers. They are not prepared for service and render none. They are nonentities in the work of Christ.

Power

The translation "be strengthened" is much weaker than the Greek original *endunamou* (present passive imperative of *endunamoō*, a causative verb to empower, to put power or strength into). Paul employs it three times in the active in a vivid personal sense of Christ as the one who empowers him. This is evident in Philippians 4:13: "I have strength for all things in the one who keeps on empowering me *[en tōi endunamounti me]*." Christ is the dynamo of energy for Paul and he has strength or power for all things so long as he is in contact with Christ. This simple fact is the secret of the tremendous dynamic energy in Paul's ministry. In 1 Timothy 1:12 Paul says: "I am grateful to Christ Jesus our Lord who did empower me *[tōi endunamōsanti me]*," when Jesus seized him on the way to Damascus and turned his life clean around (Phil. 3:12). Once more in his last epistle (2 Tim. 4:17) Paul says: "The Lord stood by me *[moi parestē]* and empowered me *[kai enedunamōsen me]*." This happened at the last trial in Rome when all had deserted him.

Paul by experience knew what it was for the Lord Jesus to stand by his side in the hour of peril. He exhorts Timothy therefore "to keep in touch with the power in the grace in Christ Jesus." Christ for Timothy, as for Paul, is the only source of power. This is the lesson that every preacher has to learn. We read sometimes of Jesus that the power of God was with Him to heal and at others that Jesus felt power gone forth from Him (Mark 5:30). Certainly no preacher has the power of God when he is out of touch with Christ. The old preachers used to talk about having liberty in preaching. The Spirit of God was with them on such occasions. The nine disciples who had failed to cast the demon out of the epileptic boy afterward asked Jesus privately: "Why could not we cast it out?" (Matt. 17:19). Two answers are given by Jesus: one the lack of faith (Matt. 17:20), the other lack of prayer (Mark 9: 29). Both are true. These very apostles on the tour of Galilee when they were sent out by twos did cast out demons; but now, at the foot of the Mount of Transfiguration, they neglected to pray and thus get in touch with God. A prayerless preacher is always a powerless preacher. Many a preacher knows what it is to fail with the very sermon that once was greatly blessed. He neglected to get in touch with God by prayer. He was not anointed with the Holy Spirit.

Electricity in modern life is a superb illustration of what Paul is here urging upon Timothy. The power in the electric street cars is not in the track, the car, the motorman, the conductor, or the copper wire, though all these are necessary. The electricity is carried by the wire, but the wire is dead without it. With it there is a live wire and the car moves. Without the electric current the car stops. Fine churches, organs, choirs, pulpits, and preachers are all excellent, but without the power of the Holy Spirit they are all sounding brass and tinkling cymbals. Once, when I was a student at Wake Forest College, the professor of electricity asked me to step upon a small table with four glass rollers so that it was insulated. Then he turned electricity on me until my hair stood on end and my clothing would pop and snap with sparks of electricity. The class was asked to come around and poke their fingers within a few inches of me but without touching me. When they did so, sparks flashed from me to their fingertips. I was electrified, charged with power. Alas that it should be so, but sometimes no power goes out from us for there is no power in us. We are not in tune with the Infinite. We are not filled with the Holy Spirit.

The scientific word for God is Energy. Paul describes God as "the one who energizes *[ho energōn]* in you both the willing and the energizing of his good pleasure" (Phil. 2:13). Great scientists like Jeans and Eddington are willing to recognize God as the primal force in all nature. That is true in every phase of life as men are at last coming to see. It is preeminently true of the life of the Christian. Thus alone shall a revival come when cold and indifferent disciples come back to God in Christ and get in touch with the Holy Spirit. Then they can touch other lives with real results. They can kindle other fires because they themselves have been rekindled at the altar of God.

Deposit

The word for deposit is an old verb for placing beside *(para)*. It is common for placing food beside one as when the five thousand were fed (Mark 6:41; Luke 9:16) and the four thousand (Mark 8:6ff.), or on the table beside one (Acts 16:34). Then the word takes the turn of depositing a trust with one for security as with a bank (Luke 12:48). The papyri have it for depositing claims to ownership of property or pledges or earnest of further payments. Then it is common for commending one to God for protection (Acts 14:23; 20:32). In 1 Timothy 1:18 Paul employs this verb for laying a charge on Timothy to fulfill the prophecies made in his youth. Here Timothy is urged by Paul to deposit the teachings, "what thou didst hear from me in the presence of many witnesses," "with reliable men," men who can be counted on to preserve and pass on the message of eternal life. In 1 Timothy 1:12 Paul had used this same adjective (faithful) of himself "because he counted me faithful putting me into the ministry, though formerly a blasphemer and a persecutor and injurious." Paul had tried to live up to Christ's hope concerning him and was still pressing on in pursuit of that goal (Phil. 3:12–16).

The idea of "deposit" or "trust" Paul has in a kindred word, a substantive, *parathēkē,* which means "a deposit" (or trust). In 1 Timothy 6:20 Paul pleads with Timothy: "O Timothy, guard the deposit." He enforces the exhortation by a warning in a participial clause, "Turning away from the profane babblings and oppositions of falsely named knowledge [Gnosticism, Paul means, common today also], which some professing missed the mark concerning the faith." Then again in 2 Timothy 1:12 Paul is fully persuaded that Jesus whom he has trusted "is able to guard my deposit against that day." He has no fear that Christ can fail as the banker in charge of Paul's spiritual interests. Jesus remains reliable *(pistos)* even if we are unreliable *(ei apistoumen),* "for he is not able to deny himself" (2 Tim. 2:13). No bandit, not even Satan himself, can break the combination of this divine treasury "hidden with Christ in God" (Col. 3:3). No one will be able to lay anything as a charge against God's elect or to separate them from the love of God in Christ Jesus (Rom. 8:33, 35, 39).

Once again Paul returns to the idea in 1 Timothy 6:20, the deposit that God has placed in Timothy: "Guard the noble [or beautiful] deposit through the Holy Spirit who dwells in us" (2 Tim. 1:14). God has made an investment in Timothy as in all His children. It is up to Timothy to make that investment good. We can all be grateful that God does invest His grace in such miserable sinners as we are. His lovingkindness and tender mercy deal with us in hope and confidence. That is Paul's feeling about himself as first among sinners in whom as chief Christ has shown what He can do with a specimen such as Paul was (1 Tim. 1:15ff.). Paul's idea is that, therefore, no one should be discouraged. God has a rich treasure in His saints in light—all sinners saved by grace, all monuments of mercy and love. This is one tremendous reason why it is good to see a child give his heart to Christ instead of coming, after a life wasted in sin, and offering the fragments to God. In the ruins at Carthage there has been found a child's metal bank with a coin worth some six cents. A financier has figured out that at compound interest this little coin would now be worth something in the nonillions, or more than a thousand octillions, nearer infinity than most of us can imagine. Is there any way to estimate the worth of a long life consecrated to the service of Christ?

Reduplication

These reliable men "will be able to teach others also," Paul says. So it has always been in the spread of the Gospel. One live coal sets fire to another. Andrew brings his brother Simon to Jesus. John brings James. Philip brings Nathanael. Dr. John R. Mott proved a generation ago that by one winning one the whole world could be brought to Christ in one generation. But often a whole life passes by without bringing another soul to the Master. Personal evangelism is the only way by which the Gospel can be successfully brought to the hearts of men. We need preaching, more of it and better; but the personal touch of heart to heart, of life on life is what counts most. I heard D. L. Moody say once in a sermon that he knew of more souls won to Christ by his conversation than by his preaching. And Moody was a wonderfully effective evangelist. Isaiah's lips were touched by a live coal from the altar of God and so he had a tongue of flame. Nature is prodigal in her efforts at the reproduction of life. Seeds fall everywhere, carried by the wind and finding congenial soil. Dr. W. H. Houghton of the Calvary Baptist Church in New York City once asked a prayer meeting audience of three hundred why they had come to his church. Some came because of the radio, some because of newspaper advertisements, but two hundred and fifty of the members came through personal invitations.

We should be drummers for Christ. Some men can live in a Christian community and never have a personal word spoken to them about their soul's welfare. Friends will talk about business, pleasure, politics, the weather, anything, everything, except the most important thing of all, which is taboo in many social circles and contacts. But if we are to pass on the torch of eternal life, we must keep our own torch blazing. Even if we do not always light that of our neighbors and friends, we can keep it burning as a witness for Christ. John the Baptist was called by Jesus "the bright and shining light" (John 5:35). We may not be so bright a light as was John, but we are expected to keep even the lower lights burning. We are all lights for Christ to the world (Matt. 5:14). If men in darkness turn to us for light and find the light gone out, we can give no witness and no help. John McCrae in "In Flanders Fields" has a word for us:

> To you from failing hands we throw
> The torch; be yours to hold it high.